21st Century Skills for Non-Profit Managers

21st Century Skills for Non-Profit Managers

A Practical Guide on Leadership and Management

Don Macdonald

21st Century Skills for Non-Profit Managers: A Practical Guide on Leadership and Management

First published in 2018 by
Business Expert Press, LLC
222 East 46th Street, New York, NY 10017
www.businessexpertpress.com

ISBN-13: 978-1-94709-818-3 (paperback)
ISBN-13: 978-1-94709-819-0 (e-book)

Business Expert Press Human Resource Management and Organizational Behavior Collection

Collection ISSN: 1946-5637 (print)
Collection ISSN: 1946-5645 (electronic)

Cover and interior design by Exeter Premedia Services Private Ltd., Chennai, India

First edition: 2018

10 9 8 7 6 5 4 3 2 1

Printed in the United States of America.

This book is dedicated to my children, Lisa and Daniel, and grandchildren, Stanley and Margot, who are the future. Any royalties go to two UK charities, Clore Social Leadership and London Football Journeys.

Abstract

Over the last 30 years nonprofit organizations have grown massively in capacity, scope, and authority right across the world. There is a growing demand for services so there are numerous opportunities for nonprofits to respond innovatively and sustainably.

If you are an experienced nonprofit manager, you will know the role is sometimes frustrating but always exhilarating, involving work with people, guiding their ideas and energy and empowering them. Severe funding cuts since the recession make this even more testing, but new prospects are also opening up.

If you are new to the management role or the sector, you need a practical book describing good practice to guide you through the issues and problems. If you manage a small nonprofit, you have to multitask, manage your time and prioritize different tasks. If you have taken on extra responsibilities, you need new skills and knowledge such as how to generate funding.

This book covers all essential aspects (staffing, communications, charity governance, donations, corporate social responsibility, crowdfunding). It contains useful case studies, resources and links, but avoids jargon and intellectualizing. Topics include how to prepare a successful business plan, empower staff and clients, write a successful fundraising application to a trust, or prepare and submit a tender to the U.S. state governments or the UK National Health Service. There is something of use for everyone.

Don has used his experience as a nonprofit manager, volunteer, staffer, fundraiser, trustee and consultant, along with his time overseeing community project funding; so as a gamekeeper turned poacher. This makes the book relevant, topical, and helpful.

Keywords

business ethics, charity donation, charity, competitive tendering, corporate social responsibility, crowdfunding, development, diversity, education, empowerment, evaluation, fundraising, general and human resource management, grant making, green environment, health, investment, leadership, management, NHS, nonprofit organizations, philanthropy, policy, project management, public, social enterprise, social, sustainability, sustainable

Contents

Preface

"In the last decades, the activity and influence of nonprofit organizations in almost every country in the world have grown exponentially" as John Casey has written.[1] In the United States, with a population of 318 million, there are over 1.5 million registered nonprofit organizations including 1,097,689 public charities, with nonprofit employment representing 10.1 percent of total employment in the United States in 2010. In the United Kingdom, with a population of 64 million (2013), around 166,000 charities are registered with the Charity Commission (2016), with the social sector bigger than the motor industry. I concentrate on these two countries for two reasons; the United States has the biggest and most influential nonprofit sector, while I developed my skills and expertise in the United Kingdom (though also working in Asia and Europe). The United States and United Kingdom also share a wide range of nonprofit organizations, cultural attributes and management expertise.

Managing nonprofit organizations is always exhilarating and sometimes frustrating, as it involves working with people at the same time as guiding their ideas and energy while empowering them. However severe funding cuts since the recession makes this even more testing. Leadership and management skills therefore become more important, yet more demanding. Hence the need for a practical book directed at managers, who may be new to the sector or taking on additional responsibilities, thus needing further skills. I have tried to avoid jargons. Readers will have a wide range of previous experience and knowledge; thus the information and concepts may seem too simplistic for some, but irrelevant for others; hopefully there is something of use for everyone, even though people will have differing points of view from me.

---

[1] https://js.sagamorepub.com/jnel/article/download/7583/5732)

I cover all essential aspects, with useful resources and links. I have mainly used my experience as a manager in the nonprofit sector, but also my time as a volunteer, staffer, fundraiser, trustee, and consultant, and even my time in two local authorities, overseeing community project funding; so as a gamekeeper turned poacher.

—Don Macdonald
July 17, 2017

Acknowledgments

Shaks Ghosh from the UK Clore Social Leadership Charity encouraged me to write this book and kept this up over the last eighteen months of its gestation. In two chapters, I needed additional expertise, so Charles Oham (Service Planning, Monitoring, Evaluating and Improving a Not for Profit Organization) and Sue Causton (Equal Opportunity, Diversity and Service User Involvement) have cowritten two chapters while Chris Durkin and Kemal Ahson helped with sections. Charles-Antoine Arnaud and Laurel Dutcher both read the whole book, making useful suggestions, while Judith Edwards, Linbert Spencer, Daniel Dumoulin, and David Tyler all checked different chapters. As ever, my wife Kate has been long-suffering and supportive; as an experienced public sector manager herself, she contributed feedback and ideas.

INTRODUCTION

Leadership and Management in Nonprofit Organizations

Don Macdonald

"Today, nonprofit organizations in the United States control upward of $1.5 trillion in assets and are increasingly relied upon to help address society's ills" according to a McKinsey report.[1] "In the last decades, the activity and influence of nonprofit organizations in almost every country in the world have grown exponentially. Nonprofits have become central to policy making, the promotion of civic action, and the delivery of new quasi-public services."[2] Nonprofits operate in an ever-changing world with increasing pressures, hence the need for relevant skills and knowledge for new managers and leaders, which this book attempts to provide.

Definitions and Numbers

Nonprofit organizations are described in different ways, including social organizations, Community and Voluntary Organizations (CVOs), Non-Governmental Organizations (NGOs), and Third Sector Organizations. The sector itself is very varied, even if I ignore all those nonprofit organizations, which are just informal associations and should not require management. I concentrate on those organizations that have been formally constituted in some way or other, such as registered charities and nonprofit companies.

This definition would still encompass tiny nonprofits with only a few volunteers offering a part-time service and on the other hand enormous

---

[1] http://mckinsey.com/industries/social-sector/our-insights/the-dynamic-nonprofit-board

[2] https://js.sagamorepub.com/jnel/article/download/7583/5732)

social enterprises, with hundreds of professional staff, competing for government contracts to deliver social objectives.

Private companies provide services to deliver social objectives, but they are different because they aim to make a profit from those services to go to shareholders. So the definition of a nonprofit organization is that the service must be oriented toward social objectives, with any surpluses invested back into services, the community, or some other public benefit. There are also numerous educational charities, such as schools and universities, which I am not covering because their objectives are primarily educational rather than social, even though there are overlaps between the two areas.

The original nonprofit organizations in Europe were church based, many of which survive in Europe such as Santa Casa de Misericórdia, founded in Portugal in 1498. In the United States (U.S.) in 1739 George Whitefield set up the first charity, Bethesda, an orphanage, while Thomas Coram's Foundling Hospital was the first secular charity in the United Kingdom (UK) in the same year. "In the 1830s the French observer…. de Tocqueville noted Americans' remarkable propensity for forming and joining associations."[3] The great expansion of charities in both countries came in the Victorian age, with the founding of the YMCA, Salvation Army, Red Cross and many others. In the UK in 1948, when the National Health Service (NHS) was introduced, around 25 percent of the hospitals were still managed by charities.

Types of Nonprofit Organizations

Charles Handy listed five types of nonprofit organizations:

- Service providers
- Research and advocacy organizations
- Self-help groups
- Intermediary bodies
- Those that fall into more than one category[4]

---

[3] https://www.penguin.co.uk/books/56324/america-empire-of-liberty

[4] Handy, C. 1988. *Understanding Voluntary Organizations: How to Make Them Function Effectively.* Penguin.

Chris Durkin believes it is the clear value base and social mission that distinguishes nonprofit organizations from other types of organizations.[5]

In addition, there are a range of different governance structures utilized by different nonprofit organizations; some register as charities, some as limited companies with charitable objectives and some as cooperatives (see Governance chapter). Some operate within one country, others internationally, in countries where "the majority of the population lives in poverty (while) the state does not provide reliable public services or protect citizens."[6] There is also a distinction between those nonprofit organizations providing services and others, such as the Bill and Melinda Gates Foundation, which give grants to other nonprofit organizations to carry out work.

As one commentator wrote, the U.S. has a long history of smaller government, lower welfare spending and strong nonprofits, whereas other countries, such as Australia, Canada, and the UK, have combined liberalism with the development of stronger welfare state provisions in the early to mid-20th century.

Funding

The top four countries in terms of charitable giving by individuals as a percentage of GDP are the U.S. (1.44 percent), New Zealand (0.79 percent), Canada (0.77 percent), and the UK (0.54 percent), whereas it was only 0.12 percent in Japan. In the U.S. and Australia, where donation statistics are divided by sector, approximately one-third of all private donations go to religious organizations.

U.S. Nonprofit Organizations

In the U.S. with a population of 318 million, there are more than 1.5 million registered nonprofit organizations including: 1,097,689 public charities, 105,030 private foundations and 68,337 other types of nonprofit organizations, such as chambers of commerce, fraternal and

---

[5] E-mail to author 2016.

[6] John Casey file:///C:/Users/DONMAC~1.COM/AppData/Local/Temp/7583-24809-1-PB.pdf

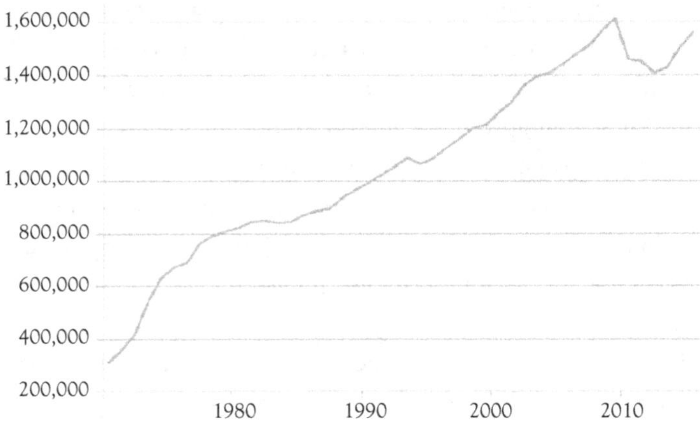

Figure I.1 The growth of registered nonprofits in the United States

civic organizations.[7] The sector has grown rapidly but consistently over the last 40 years, as shown by Figure I.1, though large numbers close each year according to the U.S. Internal Revenue.

U.S. Staffing and Volunteering

According to a 2012 report by the Center for Civil Society Studies (John Hopkins University), nonprofit employment represented 10.1 percent of total employment in the U.S., with employees totaling 10.7 million. The nonprofit workforce is the third largest of all U.S. industries behind retail trade and manufacturing.

Nonprofit employment by sector is approximately 57 percent for health services, 15 percent for education, 13 percent for social assistance, 7 percent for civic associations, 4 percent for other, 3 percent for arts culture, and 2 percent for professional services. Around 25.3 percent of Americans over the age of 16 volunteered through or for an organization between September 2010 and September 2014.

United Kingdom Numbers

In the UK with a population of 64 million (2013), there are around 166,000 charities registered with the Charity Commission in 2016, most

[7] http://nccs.urban.org/data-statistics/quick-facts-about-nonprofits

of which are small with about 50 percent having an annual income under £10,000 and around 80 percent under £100,000.[8] There are around 70,000 social enterprises (Social Enterprise UK), some also registered as charities. Around 100,000 nonprofit organizations are not formally incorporated as companies or charities.[9] What can be seen from these figures is that the majority of UK nonprofits are very small, locally focused, and "staffed" by volunteers.

Big household names in the UK, such as Cancer Research UK, Save the Children International and British Red Cross with annual incomes above £10m, make up less than 1 percent of UK charities, yet these few hundred account for almost 50 percent of the total income.

Whatever the size of the nonprofit sector, it is much smaller than the private or public sectors. Some suggest that the traditional dividing line between sectors may be breaking down, but to me it seems that there may just be greater interchange of ideas and people; the nonprofit sector is still so much smaller than other sectors.

UK Staffing and Volunteering

According to the NCVO approximately 800,000 people were employed in the nonprofit sector in the UK by the end of 2012, equaling approximately 648,000 full-time equivalent staff. Since 2002, the nonprofit workforce has seen an overall increase of around 234,000 employees (41 percent), with a dip during 2010 to 2011. As a proportion of the total UK workforce, it has risen from 2.1 percent to roughly 2.7 percent during this time. More than two-third (68 percent) of the nonprofit workforce were women compared with the public sector (64 percent) and private sector (39 percent).

In August 2012 through April 2013, 29 percent of adults in England (the largest UK country) said that they had formally volunteered at least once a month in the previous year, and 44 percent said that they had volunteered at least once in that year. This equates to around 12.7 million

[8] https://data.ncvo.org.uk/

[9] Knight, B. 1993. *Voluntary Action*. London: Centris.

people volunteering in England once a month, and 19.2 million once a year (NCVO).[10]

Context

The current context in which nonprofit organizations managers operate is both challenging and demanding. In the last 50 years (since the author started volunteering for a charity, while still at school), the most important issues include the rise of feminism and women's rights, the fact that human rights issues have become much higher profile, with disabled people and other minority groups demanding greater rights, while gaining greater access and support, which continues in spite of recent spending cuts.

Diversity issues have become far more important, with the legalization of homosexuality and eventually same sex marriage. The U.S. population is growing slowly, while the UK population is growing apace, with both more children and an aging population, with a consistent rise in non-native born residents, particularly European in the last 10 years. In the U.S. and UK, while Anglican Church attendance has declined, other Pentecostal Christian churches and religions report increased attendances.

There is much less deference across the whole of society; service users' views are taken much more into account by nonprofit organizations and government itself. Nonprofits have become much more professional, along with an enormous expansion of private companies supporting the charitable sector, on everything including IT, fundraising, and HR.

Standards of living increased steadily over the last 50 years until the 2008 recession, although enormous wealth gaps exist, along with poverty for certain groups; for example, those suffering benefit cuts. Vastly increased numbers go to university. Family structures have changed, with more people living together and bearing children before marriage, which then happens at an older age.

With financial deregulation, globalization has increased, with a huge decline in UK and U.S. heavy industries, a fall in manufacturing employment, a growth in UK and U.S. service industries and an enormous

---

[10] https://data.ncvo.org.uk/a/almanac14/how-many-people-regularly-volunteer-in-the-uk-3

increase in the power of multinational corporations. While there has been a growth in employment rights, this has been accompanied by a growth in zero hours' contracts and part-time jobs. There is much more international travel and a growth in international charities, which must be linked.

The rise of the contract culture and the introduction of privatization has been profound across many sectors, including railways, and utilities (UK) and prison services. It has led to an increase in private sector organizations delivering health and social care, community health services and unemployment support in the UK; this has been so profound that this has been described as "a shadow state," with companies too pervasive to be allowed to fail.[11]

Possibly the most significant change is the arrival of the digital age and social media, with immense changes in how we communicate, work and entertain ourselves. So it is rather unclear what will happen in the next 5 years, let alone the next 50 years.

Opportunities

The current situation for nonprofit organizations is both very pressurized but with numerous opportunities opening up, including:

- New issues being tackled, with growth in medical charities and those protecting the environment.
- With aging populations, demand is increasing all the time for care, with opportunities for innovative nonprofits.
- New organizations develop, offering new ways of tackling social problems; for example, online counseling or mass movements like Change.org.
- A great deal of self-help provision is being set up, empowering patients' groups, minority, and faith groups along with a continuing involvement from idealistic young people.
- New forms of funding, such as crowdfunding, encourage innovation.

---

[11] http://socialenterprise.org.uk/uploads/files/2012/12/the_shadow_state_3_dec1.pdf

- Online communication encourages a greater interchange of ideas, training, and support, particularly across national boundaries (for example, LinkedIn).
- Corporate Social Responsibility (CSR) is increasing. Commercial companies are now judged by the public on issues including their ethical treatment of staff (Nike "slave wages"), sustainability and environmental footprints (BP), work practices (Uber), and payment of tax (Google, Amazon). This makes for more of a level playing field if nonprofit organizations are competing for contracts with the private sector.

Pressures

On the other hand, there are numerous pressures on nonprofit organizations:

- Social problems (for example, inequality, racial discrimination, youth unemployment, mental health issues, and substance abuse) continue to prevail, though for a time crime appeared to be reducing in the UK even though prison numbers increased.
- Government spending cuts continue. UK nonprofits are more dependent on this source than U.S. nonprofits, thus the biggest ever squeeze in UK government grants has hit small organizations hardest.[12]
- There has been a huge increase in competitive tendering and commissioning; in these competitions, small nonprofits find it hard to compete, so in many cases the results have led to nonprofits being undercut by organizations using fewer, less qualified and cheaper staff, or a reduction in service quality, with some nonprofits taking on contracts they cannot deliver properly.
- Government, at all levels, have introduced policies of tendering out bigger contracts, which excludes most smaller nonprofits; even in tendering consortium led by the private

[12] http://ncvo.org.uk/images/documents/policy_and_research/funding/financial-trends-for-small-and-medium-sized-charities-ncvo-lloyds-bank-foundation-2016.pdf

sector, many nonprofits complained they were just used as bid candy by private sector companies.[13]

- Investigative reporting revealed that hundreds of charities out of over one million registered charities in the U.S. raised millions of dollars each year but siphoned most into large salaries and contracts with companies owned by friends and relatives.[14] Research in the U.S. suggests that one in three people do not trust in charities, with sociologists in the 1990s detecting "a marked decline in church going, union membership and involvement in school PTAs" and other nonprofits.[15]
- Large UK charities are currently being heavily criticized, over a range of issues. Research for the UK Charity Commission[16] reports that public trust and confidence in UK charities has fallen to the lowest level since 2005. This is based on criticism of high salaries for senior staff and fundraising methods (for example, excessive mailing and phone calls).

Management

Management itself is a skill, but it is not an exact science as it involves working with people. Bookshops now stock shelves of management books though most are about private sector management, but issues facing nonprofit managers are very different.

There is no agreed bottom line in nonprofit work, in the way that profit supplies this in the private sector. So there is often disagreement about objectives and methods, or a lack of agreement at all levels, which requires more work to achieve a consensus and proper understanding. Sometimes these disagreements are papered over, leaving a lack of clarity about objectives. An example of this is the way that the UK Anglican Church com-

---

13 https://theguardian.com/society/patrick-butler-cuts-blog/2011/jun/22/bid-candy-charities-carved-out-of-work-program

14 http://cironline.org/americasworstcharities

15 https://www.penguin.co.uk/books/56324/america-empire-of-liberty

16 https://gov.uk/government/uploads/system/uploads/attachment_data/file/284712/ptc_survey_2010.PDF

promises on decisions about same sex marriage. Many experts believe that fudge and compromise are more prevalent in the nonprofit sector.

Most nonprofits are competitive with their rivals, of any size or sector, for funding, influence, and public attention. Small charities have recently been criticized in the UK for not merging or at least sharing more back-room services. In my view this is only partially fair since most small nonprofits compensate for their size with greater cost-effectiveness. Secular minority nonprofits in the UK have achieved a great deal locally, but not to the same extent nationally, compared to the influence developed by minority religious groups.

All UK governments since 2009 have tried to encourage social enterprise opt-outs but this has proved relatively slow to take off, probably because of staff fears about pensions in the NHS and the emphasis placed on social finance based on loans, which is avoided by most nonprofits because of the risks involved.

Management in the nonprofit sector is subject to different influences from the private sector; an example is that there are more stakeholders, such as donors and beneficiaries. In turn the media also become involved and comment. One significant group of stakeholders are volunteers, vastly more of whom are involved at all levels than in the public or private sectors, even though the influence of professionals prevails in the large nonprofits.

The financial squeeze on nonprofits has created enormous tension between managing flexibility, quality, and affordability as Naomi Eisenstadt, a Scottish Government adviser, stated.[17] Nonprofit management can be likened to a roller coaster ride, with all the highs and lows, which makes it essential that nonprofit managers keep informed, while learning new skills. This book covers the key issues, analyzes essential concepts, while providing relevant and useful advice and information on how to provide good management and leadership. However the issues are so important and the situation changes so often, that it is crucial that people make use of training and coaching, on an ongoing basis, to assist them in planning a way forward in their management roles, coping with change while making a success of their organization.

---

[17] https://theguardian.com/society/2016/sep/06/naomi-eisenstadt-poverty-adviser-to-nicola-sturgeon

CHAPTER 1

Good Practice in Leadership and Management

Don Macdonald

Overview

This chapter examines good practice of leadership and management, discussing the qualities and skills required to act as the senior manager of a nonprofit sector organization. More is described in Chapters 7 and 9.

Introduction

This chapter concentrates on the attributes required as the senior manager of a nonprofit organization, either an independent organization or one operating within a larger entity. Professional management standards and literature are drawn on. However it has also been relevant to draw on 25 years' practical management experience on the ground, feedback from colleagues and coaches and the actual experience of being managed, to identify the essential competences.

Background to Nonprofit Organization Management

The role of the senior manager is very different within a small nonprofit organization, with different skills required, more management necessary, while significant service delivery expertise is required as there are no cohorts of service experts in support.

Specific qualities are required for managing in the nonprofit sector. Peter Drucker in a specialist book points out that nonprofit stakeholders are much more varied and important than in "the average business" (Drucker 1990). Jim Collins states there is a "diffuse power structure" in the nonprofit sector, which in turn makes management harder (Collins 2005).

Most authorities agree "the single most important determinant of the success of an organization is the quality of its leadership" (Bolton and Abdy 2007). However the job of leading an organization effectively is highly complex, with no magic formula to provide good leadership to be replicated everywhere. In fact Barbara Kellerman has written that years and years of "leadership studies" have made little progress in clarifying what leadership is or how to teach it (Kellerman 2012).

The qualities required will obviously vary considerably according to the context in which they are deployed, namely the objectives and activities of each organization, the services being provided, the organizational structure (company structure, Board setup), size (budget, staffing, numbers of team leaders), funding (contracts, grants), and organizational culture. The role of the senior manager will be critically affected by these organizational issues; for instance, in large organizations there are specialist Human Resource (HR) departments, whereas in small organizations most, or even all, of the major personnel issues have to be dealt with by the senior manager, albeit with advice.

Certain areas of specific knowledge should not be considered essential for managers, as they can be easily bought in or accessed, for example, legal knowledge, while other skills can also be learnt quickly; for example, IT spreadsheets. It is the fundamental skills and qualities of leadership and management, on which I concentrate.

Key Qualities of Leadership and Management

The following list of leadership and management competences comes from the UK Management Standards (2008). The full list stretches over many pages and they have often been adapted by organizations for their own policies: for instance, a UK college has a 13-page competency framework for managers, while nonprofits have also drawn up their own lists.

One of the summary lists gives an overview of the breadth and depth of skills and qualities required for leadership and management:

1. Create a vision of where your project is going, communicate it clearly and enthusiastically, with objectives and plans, to people in your team.
2. Ensure your people understand and see how the team's vision, objectives, and operational plans link to vision and objectives of overall organization.
3. Steer your team successfully through difficulties and challenges, including conflicts.
4. Create and maintain a culture in your team, which encourages and recognizes creativity and innovation.
5. Develop a range of leadership styles and select and apply these to appropriate situations and people.
6. Communicate regularly, making effective use of different communication methods, with all your people and show you listen to what they say.

7. Give your people support and advice when needed especially during setback and change.
8. Motivate and support your people to achieve work and development objectives and provide recognition when successful.
9. Empower your people to develop their own ways of working and take their own decisions within agreed boundaries.
10. Encourage people to give a lead in their own areas of expertise and show willingness to follow this lead.
11. Win, through your performance, the trust and support of your people for your leadership and get regular feedback on your performance.

These standards are quite general, consequently inexperienced managers may find it hard to understand exactly what they should be doing just from these. So it is important to examine key aspects and discuss how nonprofit organization managers should best implement these.

Forward Thinker

The senior manager in any organization needs to be forward thinking, with a vision of where they want the organization to go. They must act as a strategic thinker, devising a strategy for the organization (including a Vision and Mission), gain board agreement, with stakeholders and staff's views taken into consideration as well. This will set a lead as to where the organization is headed, along with communicating this to staff and stakeholders. From the strategy, an operational plan needs to be developed for staff to work to, with attainable and measurable objectives.

Conditions are changing all the time, some funding is drying up, while other opportunities appear; sometimes this is because of a change of government or policy, sometimes economic pressures, social trends, or changes in markets. An example is that with the 2008 recession followed by the change of UK government in 2010, enormous cuts in government spending were imposed in the UK, specialist contractors were squeezed out and several nonprofit training providers were bankrupted. Similar cuts in government spending happened in the United States.

So new strategies are often required to cope with change, but innovation for innovation's sake is not a good idea. Any new strategies must be carefully researched, devised, and considered, otherwise an organization can be endangered. It is quite possible for leaders to destroy a sound organization by moving into delivering impractical new services without carefully thinking through the consequences; this was demonstrated by the Novas Scarman charity's sharp decline and ultimate demise based on their leadership's bizarre strategy, inadequate governance and poor risk management (Third Sector 2010), elaborated in the following case study. Stakeholders are more important in nonprofit organizations than in private companies, where profits are the bottom line accepted by everyone; therefore stakeholders need to be consulted before major changes or innovation.

The senior manager needs to take the long view of where the organization is headed and plan ahead accordingly. This involves keeping properly informed and up-to-date about current and impending social, economic, and political policies and influences, which affect both the future direction and viability of the organization. This requires extensive reading, networking with key stakeholders, and careful planning ahead, after analyzing what risks are involved; in the 1990s one management role model told the author that good managers should read four daily newspapers to keep up-to-date with the business and political worlds; nowadays this would be done online, and one issue is making sure managers do not become overloaded with too much information.

It is essential for the manager to be objective and have a realistic view of their own organization's strengths and weaknesses and the capacity to take on any new tasks and deliver the requisite outputs. They must play the long game, rather than settle for immediate short-term gains. Longer-term thinking can too easily be overtaken by day-to-day issues in a small organization where you have less chance to delegate work to others. As Peter Drucker said "The most important task of an organization's leader is to anticipate the crisis" (Drucker 1990).

It is necessary to set aside sufficient time to ensure that rigorous thinking and planning happens; some managers use their own coaching sessions to examine difficult issues and plan ahead.

Setting an Example

Setting an example seems a very obvious requirement for managers, even though it is not included in the standards. Adults learn through example and this applies even more strongly to organizations, where organizational culture is a strong factor in determining staff behavior. Managers must consistently set an example on almost everything, thereby communicating what is and isn't permissible, what standards are required in the organization's work and probity at work; this includes working the required hours, punctuality, no phone calls in meetings, no excessive private work or communication at work, and so on.

Staff model themselves on the senior manager, who sets the tone for the whole organization. An experienced teacher once told the author that the head teacher that they most admired after 30 years school teaching was always the first into school and last to leave (Davey 2012). Another teacher, with a 40-year track record who became a manager themselves, said that their worst school principal did not set an example, carrying out little work herself, reading a trashy newspaper in her office, and leaving essential tasks to the newly qualified teachers (Mulhare 2012).

If the manager sets an example, they can then be firm and consistent about setting performance standards throughout the organization. They can set the right tone, encourage high standard work, praise the work of the best staff and hold them up as exemplars, without showing favoritism, and so improve performance throughout the organization. It is also important to set boundaries on how close managers get to staff on a personal level, which can be hard especially in small, friendly organizations; but it helps maintain objectivity and avoids the dangers of favoritism being perceived by staff.

Motivating and Developing Staff

A manager must motivate their staff, although charismatic leadership is overrated.[1] Managers should support their staff, who are the ones

---

[1] www.forbes.com/sites/adigaskell/2017/05/31/should-we-beware-charismatic-leaders/#7b39f58a27df

delivering services or working with clients or customers. Managers must set clear roles and responsibilities for each team member, so that it is obvious what is expected of them in terms of tasks, objectives, and standards.

On the other hand managers must not micromanage staff, watching too closely over results or directing operations in detail. This stultifies development and innovation, while senior managers should have more important things to do with their own time. The use of mobile phones enables staff to consult managers on difficult issues if necessary. Managers must encourage initiative among staff in a progressive way, encouraging them to use their own judgment more and more, even allowing them to make mistakes, from which they learn. Like a good parent the manager's job is done if staff can operate successfully and autonomously.

Managers should make time to listen to staff and hear their concerns and ambitions, coaching staff to improve performance; encouraging staff to produce their own solutions to problems is more effective than telling staff what to do; putting time into learning coaching skills is invaluable for managers.

A lesson I learnt from my youth work was never to give an instruction that there is no chance of being obeyed (I subsequently discovered that this is also a guiding maxim in the armed services). Also managers should never ask staff to do anything they would not be prepared to do themselves. As staff become more experienced they should be empowered and given more responsibility as per situational leadership theory, proposed by Adair (Adair 1988) along with Hersey, and Blanchard (shown in Figure 1.1). Clearly the responsibility levels allowed to staff by the senior

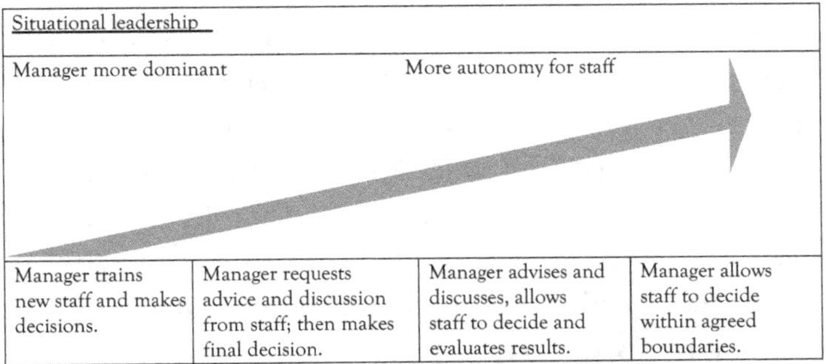

Figure 1.1 Situational leadership

manager depends on the experience and skills of the staff concerned and the importance of the task undertaken.

Getting the Priorities Right

Balancing all the different aspects of management can be difficult but it is essential that managers think straight and get their priorities right. Time management is critical for managers but harder in small nonprofits where managers must multitask. As most nonprofits are small, the roles of senior leader and operational manager are invariably combined, while in bigger organizations the leader or CEO delegates day-to-day management to other managers, leaving more time for the leadership role. Without this separation of roles, difficulties arise; "Small businesses have been characterized by their lack of resources, lack of systems and largely idiosyncratic approach to management" (Mazzarol), which is as true for small nonprofits.

Managers of all size organizations can allow their priorities to become distorted, if they become bogged down in the wrong tasks. In large organizations particularly, the requirements of legislation and red tape, including health and safety, risk assessments, HR issues, often overwhelm and distract managers from concentrating on essential management. So prioritizing one's tasks and time is essential (see Chapter 9).

Managers just working longer and longer hours does not help, nor working on activities with no clear understanding of their value to the organization; one example is the endless round of lengthy meetings, another is any interagency partnership, hamstrung by squabbling. There can be a danger of "substituting acquaintance for knowledge, activity for understanding, reporting for analysis, quantity of work for quality" as a senior UK ambassador once wrote perceptively (Meyer 2012).

Managers must deal with the necessary paper work efficiently, completing the necessary reports on staff, operations and funding, but must not let it take over their real work. Parkinson's Law, "Work expands to meet the time available," can be very dangerous. Missing deadlines for funding bids or sending returns in late to funders or government affects the organization's budget and reputation or both, while keeping staff waiting for expenses loses their loyalty.

Balancing these different priorities and completing the tasks can be difficult; John Adair's concept of overlapping management tasks (Adair

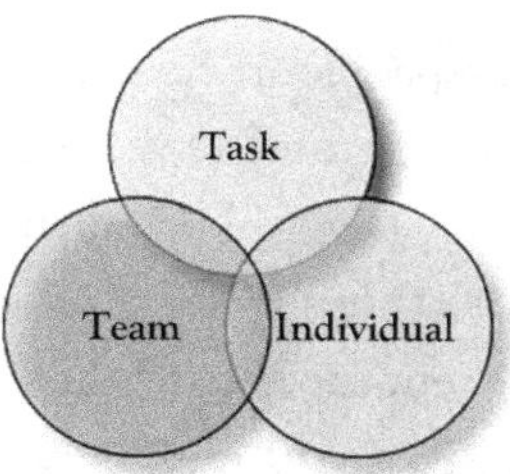

Figure 1.2 Overlapping leadership tasks

1973) is very relevant to most manager, who are continually having to juggle different priorities (see Figure 1.2).

Entrepreneurial

The senior manager needs to be proactive, creative, and innovative, open to new ideas, evaluating the relevance and applicability of new opportunities and able to introduce new services successfully. Even in the charitable sector, managers need to be entrepreneurial, always on the lookout to make new contacts, to find and utilize new openings and raise funds for new projects and services. It is important that organizations are not skewed toward delivering unsuitable or unsustainable services solely in the pursuit of funds; however if the right level of resources is offered that fit with the organization's strategy, then it is wise to follow up funding offers. Entrepreneurialism should be based on a realistic assessment and understanding of the state of the opportunities, proper risk assessment and an analysis of the returns from contracts and the capability of the particular organization managers are leading. Decision making is an absolutely crucial skill, and there are techniques available for managers to improve their ability in this area, such as coaching, as well as training. The Novas Scarman case study illustrates where due process was not followed and a viable organization was destroyed.

Case Study: The Demise of Novas Scarman

The initial genesis of the UK Novas Group in 1998 seemed both sensible and innovative as it merged three small charities providing care and housing to homeless people in London, Northern Ireland, and Liverpool, creating a much more effective organization, as at that time homeless charities were too small. Novas then expanded its provision into other towns with 2,000 housing units across the United Kingdom which stretched management capacity further.

In 2006 it was planning a £50 million redevelopment of its hostels and housing provision, but a Housing Corporation report of June 2006 warned that its proposed redevelopment could prove too ambitious as it lacked proper development capacity at this scale.

In 2004 Novas merged with Scarman Trust, a regeneration charity, and, as part of the hostel redevelopment, it then embarked on a highly ambitious arts center development. Arts funding in the United Kingdom provided much lower incomes when compared with running hostels, where 40 percent of the income came from government subsidies and was topped up with another 40 percent of government grants. In addition the steady increase in property prices in the United Kingdom, particularly in London, increased the asset base of hostel nonprofits, which owned their hostels, like Novas.

These difficulties were compounded by developing two arts centers in two different cities, with the Liverpool one costing £17 million, albeit with £6.5 regeneration grants. In addition the founding CEO, who also sat on the board, embarked on an expensive spree buying antique fittings, Malaysian art and other fripperies, exposed in a government agency investigation and publicized in the Daily Telegraph and he was forced out. The report raised concerns over "alleged cronyism, nepotism bullying, and mismanagement."

A new board was appointed in 2009 after the investigation. Novas had to sell a large number of properties to its competitors, but still failed to sort out its finances and eventually had to sell its flagship, Arlington House, where George Orwell stayed in the 1930s. The organization was holed under the waterline by the time a new chair and CEO were appointed and the organization was relaunched as People Can in 2010. The pension commitments of £17 million were too great, the charity was wound up in 2012 and almost 300 staff lost their jobs.

One could conclude that some government grants would be so heavily cut back that it was wise for Novas Scarman to try to reduce dependency on these and switch to more trading and other activity. However, the lessons are that organizations should not be led into a new risky business area, if they have insufficient knowledge or experience to embark on this, when they have not fully researched the venture and assessed the risks of damaging an existing and stable organization. The move by Novas Scarman seems an example of "mission creep," venturing into the unknown, without any clear evidence that this would benefit either the clients or the organization, set up to serve them. The regulator stated there were failures in management and clearly there was over-reliance on and lack of supervision of the charismatic founder; the new chair said the real lesson to organizations was that risk management and the ability to look at real case scenarios were critically important.

Communication Skills

Communication skills for managers include written and verbal skills obviously, but also networking and partnership skills. Most managers are stronger in certain areas of communication than others; a respected colleague once told me that a visionary manager, who founded three renowned UK charities which contribute enormously and still flourish 50 years afterwards, was no good in one-to-one situations with staff. (Later I discovered that his wife cofounded these charities and presumably supplied the necessary soft skills.) The converse can also apply, where a senior manager is good at one to ones with people but lacks drive or the ability to communicate with large numbers.

External networking is another necessary skill, including presenting a positive picture of the organization through conferences, articles, and presentations. Networking can also ensure that the organization's tenders or bids do not land cold on someone's desk but with a favorable impression already created.

In large organizations with numerous different departments, it is also necessary to network internally with colleagues to proceed more effectively and swiftly; for example, securing publicity for a project, ensuring a team's jobs are advertised quickly, sorting your IT problems ASAP, or keeping the health and safety inspector happy. In many respects this is like carrying out community work but in the organization. This requires taking time out to get to know key staff, to find out how different staff perform and to make positive relationships with staff in key nonservice departments; for example, finance, HR, IT, and so on. This is particularly important in large organizations or those with head offices, which do not always have an adequate understanding of the issues facing frontline staff, particularly those hundreds of miles away.

Productive Relationships

The manager needs to build and maintain a range of constructive and positive relationships externally with potential customers, commissioners and funders, and potential partner organizations, through networking. It is far, far easier to become part of consortia bidding for contracts than going through the whole time-consuming process of tendering on your own, particularly as small organizations new to tendering lack both a track record and bidding expertise. This process is also likely to be more successful since partnerships are fashionable, the minimum size of contracts on some UK government tenders is high, often £1 million, and most tenders do not allow an organization to bid for more than 40 or 50 percent of current turnover. To be included in a consortium requires networking and your organization meeting certain standards (see Chapter 4).

Partnerships are being encouraged at many different levels; so skills in this area are also important, as your organization may be required to work with other delivery partners in a consortium or with a funder who wants to be involved in how the work is presented or publicized. Qualities required are tact, diplomacy, and patience.

Resilience and Adaptability

Resilience and adaptability are other important qualities, as the unexpected will arrive to confront the organization. These qualities are not always included on the lists of required qualities of managers and leaders yet it is absolutely crucial. All organizations face downturns and setbacks, not within their control, however much risk planning is in place. I agree with Murphy's Law, which states if something can go wrong, it will, however many precautions have been put in place.

It is essential for leaders to be resilient, to demonstrate their resilience to the team and to lead the organization to overcome the setbacks. This is emphasized by one of the most prescient commentators on the most recent financial crash, Nassim Taleb (Taleb 2012), who describes the importance of a quality he designates as antifragility, which leaders need to deploy to ensure that their organizations become and stay resilient. Adaptability I see as the quality of making good, after something has gone awry.

Case Study

A new community project was set up for young offenders as an alternative to youth custody sentences and project went well for the first few months. One night after group work run by the least experienced staff member, some young men broke back into the day center, overcoming the burglar alarms, stealing the project minibus, photocopier, and much other equipment. The theft was not discovered until the next day and the demoralized staff were stunned and confused about what needed to be done, both with regard to practical steps, understanding the motives of the young people involved and feeling motivated. The manager was upset by the incident, but they had experienced several similar incidents previously in other projects. So the manager took the lead, instigating a review of work practices, improving security and working with the young staff member to enable them to understand what had really happened and the reasons for this.

This resilience and adaptability enables managers to deal with, not avoid, unpleasant or fraught situations. Providing services to clients and customers in the community makes organizations potentially vulnerable to complaints, issues, and problems thrown up by relations with clients or customers or with regulators and commissioners, which must be dealt with effectively and in a short time scale, otherwise adverse comment or publicity can ensue and affect the organization's standing; the UK Kids'

Company charity was wound up after a complaint about abuse of a client triggered greater scrutiny of its finances and management; subsequently the abuse story proved unfounded but by that stage the mismanagement was clear to all.

Expertise in Operations

The senior manager must be perceptive, with a certain level of intellect and intellectual curiosity rather than intellectual brilliance. They must have experience in and knowledge of their specific profession or industry, sufficient to provide relevant leadership, with good understanding of the services they are providing and the markets they are tackling.

According to research (Goodall 2012), organizations run by expert leaders—those with deep technical knowledge and experience in the organization's core business—perform better than those organizations where general managers are in charge. The expert leaders make better managers because of their deep-rooted technical knowledge, which helps them devise and implement more effective and intuitive strategies. This expertise enables them to manage in a more sophisticated way, rather than just relying on crude numerical targets. Also the managers' own track record and reputation in turn helps recruit and retain other talented staff.

The use of IT has spread rapidly, particularly the Internet, which is now being used for promoting organizations and fundraising. In addition more online data and reporting systems are being used to capture and report on information about service outputs across organizations. Most applications can be learnt. But in this rapidly changing technological society, it is clear that a minimum level of IT literacy is now an essential attribute for managers. This is not just expertise in specific IT applications, such as spreadsheets or social media, but sufficient understanding to be able to make decisions with reasonable knowledge as to how IT can best help an organization.

Likewise there is a minimum level of financial skill required for all managers so that they can budget, produce accurate financial projections, understand what accounts mean and plan ahead properly. In all sectors budgets must be balanced or organizations will be wound up, resources must be shifted to relevant areas, and potential funding gaps tackled.

Unrealistic projections of income for nonprofit organizations bring organizations down. Currently the pension shortfalls have led some nonprofits to owe more in pension commitments than their current or prospective income can cover, so prudent organizations are changing their pension arrangements.

Emotional Intelligence

I am skeptical of unproven methods and their effectiveness, but it is clear that emotional intelligence and soft skills are essential qualities in managers. Ten years ago the term emotional intelligence was not used with regard to management; instead other terms such as human understanding or people skills might be used, But Dale Carnegie's famous book *How to win friends and influence people* in 1936 was an example of using soft skills. It is now accepted that emotional intelligence is an essential ingredient for managers in all sectors, This is even more true of nonprofits because they deliver social objectives and most involve providing services for people.

Even in strongly hierarchical and military organizations such as the 19th century UK Navy, leaders such as Admiral Nelson were admired for their care for their seamen (Lambert 2009). Understanding how to get the best out of their own staff is essential; one senior military officer used to visit underperforming staff in their own offices to put them at their ease (Macdonald 1982). This tactic—management by walking around—is very valid as it enables the manager to see what is really going on, gain feedback, discuss progress with staff on a more equal basis and be seen to on the frontline.

Emotional intelligence can be developed or improved by managers reflecting on their own personality, relationship, and performance. A 360-degree feedback can be a useful tool, where managers obtain feedback from both staff they manage as well their own chair or senior manager. This process can be painful for oversensitive managers so another strategy is for managers to arrange to be coached to ensure they receive feedback on their own performance, gain understanding, and become more objective.

In different management structures, there will be also specific skills managers need, for instance skills in dealing with management boards or unions may be required in those nonprofit organizations where these exist. In specific nonprofit organizations there will also be specialist service knowledge, which managers need to acquire, supervise, and challenge the specialists in their own teams.

Conclusion

The most crucial areas for management and leadership in nonprofit organization are combining an entrepreneurial quality with people skills and with experience and expertise in the specific operational area being tackled. Any competent manager will utilize entrepreneurial flair, people skills and operational experience to generate new ideas about new services from staff and others, thereby renewing services or setting up new ones.

Managers need to develop their own leadership and management style and aptitude and be confident in that. They need to learn new skills all the time and be open to new ways of working (see Chapter 7). Leadership in this ever-changing world has become more and more pressured; expectations are higher and higher to produce results. On the other hand there are more leadership training programs and coaches available to assist managers to develop their own specific leadership styles and make the grade.

To sum up leadership succinctly, here is an example from the arts field, where Deborah Bull, Creative Director of the UK Royal Opera Ballet, defined leadership as being based on hard work: "A strong sense of values, values which are derived from repeatedly working on yourself, on your profession, the sense of discipline, the sense of team work, the sense of playing the long game, the sense of learning from failure, and that constant pushing the boundaries forward while respecting the past."

Do's and Don'ts for New Leaders

1. Be positive, be resilient, and set a lead in the organization at all times.
2. Look after yourself, recruit a coach or join a support group to test out your ideas, sustaining you through the inevitable hard times.

3. Do make sure you properly understand the finances, budgets, and contracts.
4. Stay well informed and plan ahead, including analyzing the worst possible scenarios.
5. Do project a good image of your organization's work, using proper evaluation and case studies.
6. Listen to your staff; they know better than you as to what is really going on at the coal face, even though they won't always be right about what to do next.
7. Do not take any management job offered to you; find out what is really happening in the organization, its future prospects and the staff you would be managing.
8. Don't work on your own, but find key people to form a team to work with.
9. Don't boast, but do underpromise and overdeliver.
10. Don't allow your organization to be dependent on one source of income, but diversify.
11. Don't show fear and panic, however much you feel it inside, but set an example even in the most difficult of times.

References

Adair, J. 1973. *Action-Centred Leadership.* London, England: McGraw-Hill.

Adair, J. 1988. *Effective Leadership.* London, England: Pan Books.

Bolton, M., and M. Abdy. 2007. Paper for Clore Duffield Foundation http://cloreduffield.org.UK/downloads/SLPConsultationPaperJuly07.pdf

Bull, Deborah. 2013. BBC Radio 4.

Collins, J. C., and Collins, J. C. 2005. *Good to great and the social sectors: why business thinking is not the answer: a monograph to accompany.* Boulder, CO: J. Collins.

Davey, E.K.D. 2012. Personal Communication to Author.

Drucker, P. 1990. *Managing the Non-profit Organization: Practices and Principles.* New York: Harper Collins.

Goodall, Dr AH, https://scholar.google.co.uk/citations?view_op=view_citation&hl=en&user=ad0XFggAAAAJ&citation_for_view=ad0XFggAAAAJ:hqOjcs7Dif8C

Kellerman, B. 2012. *End of Leadership.* New York; Harper Collins.

Lambert, A. 2009. *Admirals*. London, England: Faber and Faber.

Macdonald, Air Vice Marshal DMT (CB, former Director General Personnel) personal communication to his son, the author 1982

Management Standards. 2008. http://management-standards.org

Mazzarol, T. http://www.emeraldinsight.com/doi/abs/10.1108/13552550310461036

Meyer, Sir Christopher, 2012, BBC Radio 4

Mulhare, K.T. 2012, personal communication to author

Taleb, N. 2012. *Antifragile: Things That Gain From Disorder*. London, England: Penguin.

Third Sector 2010. http://thirdsector.co.UK/andrew-barnett-chair-novas-scarman-group/governance/article/976364

Williams, I. 2007. "*The Nature of Highly Effective Community and Voluntary Organizations.*" http://www.dochas.ie/sites/default/files/Williams_on_Effective_CVOs.pdf

CHAPTER 2

Practical Governance in Nonprofit Organizations

Don Macdonald

Overview

This chapter is written as a practical guide to setting up a nonprofit organization, describing and analyzing different legal structures in nonprofit organizations, the management and policy roles and responsibilities for boards and staff in different organizations, along with pay ratios and financial probity.

It includes analysis of working with stakeholders, directors, committees and decision making. Finally, it covers issues such as board composition and behavior, staff policies (complaints, whistle-blowers), and senior staff pay.

It is based on evidence from a range of sources, but the chapter also reflects the author's own experience as chief executive, manager, staffer, volunteer, and trustee in a range of different nonprofit and community organizations.

Introduction

Governance could be described as the "systems and processes that ensure the overall direction, effectiveness, supervision and accountability of an organization" (Cornforth 2003). It may seem obvious but it is essential to set up a legal structure to run your nonprofit organization; otherwise, as an unincorporated association, some funding will not be available to you, while association members could be personally liable for any debts or claims.

Different factors will affect governance in different ways; long-established organizations should already have proper procedures in place, while large or complex organizations should also have more detailed procedures in place, for instance with specialist teams for issues such as safeguarding or specialist subcommittees of the board.

Most importantly the governance of a nonprofit organization should be fit for purpose in several respects. Thus the right legal structure should be selected to achieve the objectives of the organization; a nonprofit organization involved in generating most of its income through commissioning or trading would be best setting itself up as a social enterprise (see the following for the different types), while other nonprofit organizations, involved in generating income in other ways, would be best becoming a charitable organization. In addition the composition of the board should be fit for purpose and include members with the right specialist skills and knowledge (also dealt with later).

Legal Structures

A range of different legal structures can be used in different countries for setting up nonprofit organizations including:

- Registered charities and different charitable structures

- Cooperatives
- Not-for-profit companies

There are numerous legal differences and different regulators in different countries and also between different states within those countries, which must be borne in mind if you operate there.

The following Table 2.1 outlines different legal structures that can be used to operate nonprofit organizations in the United States and UK, partly derived from the book by Ridley Duff and Bull. There are organizations set up to help and support people setting up and operating not-for-profit organizations. For more information on each structure, you can access the agencies and websites listed in the table. Some agencies recommend that professional advice should be taken before adopting any one of these. It may be possible to access this advice on a pro bono or free basis from law companies.

Some registered charities also register as companies limited by guarantee to ensure that their liability is limited to a greater degree, while others will register their trading arms as limited companies. One advantage of charitable status is that some trusts and companies will only donate to registered charities. Also some national nonprofits will manage their regional branches from the center, while others with a more decentralized structure, like the YMCA, will have local chapters with greater autonomy.

Legal Requirements

It is important to note that all nonprofits are also subject to general company legislation and steps can be taken if these are not met; thus because of financial mismanagement, trustees of the failed UK charity, Kids Company, are being threatened with being banned as company directors.[1]

---

[1] http://thirdsector.co.uk/former-trustees-chief-executive-kids-company-face-disqualification-proceedings/management/article/1431316

Table 2.1 Popular legal forms for not for profits (adapted from Ridley Duff and Bull 2016)

Category	The United States	The United Kingdom
Charity, trust or foundation	1. Foundation 2. Not-for-profit corporation 3. Public benefits corporation	1. Charity 2. Charitable company 3. Charitable incorporated 4. foundation or association (CIO)
Regulating and Support Agencies	Internal Revenue Service www.irs.gov/pub/irs-tege/governance_practices.pdf National Council of Non Profits www.councilofnonprofits.org	Charity commission www.gov.UK/government/organizations/charity-commission *National Council of Voluntary Organizations* https://ncvo.org.UK
Cooperative or mutual	1. Minimum numbers varies by state 2. Cooperative society 3. Credit union 4. Solidarity co-op	1. Minimum numbers three 2. Cooperative society 3. Credit union 4. Community benefit society (formerly friendly society)
Support Agencies	Community-wealth.org http://community-wealth.org	Cooperatives UK https://UKcoop
Socially responsible businesses	1. Benefits corporation (B-Corp) 2. Private company (C3) with nonprofit trading activities 3. Low profit corporation (L3C)	1. Community interest company (CIC) 2. Private company (CLG or CLS) with social objects 3. Employee-owned business
Regulating and Support Agencies	Social Enterprise Alliance https://socialenterprise.U.S./ B Corporations https://bcorporation.net/what-are-b-corps	CIC Regulator https://gov.UK/government/organizations/office-of-the-regulator-of-community-interest-companies Social Enterprise UK www.socialenterprise.org.UK/ Social Firms UK www.socialfirmsuk.co.UK

Most Appropriate Structure

There are advantages and disadvantages for each structure. The need for good governance prevails across all different types. The most common structure for new UK social enterprises, spun out as mutuals, is the Community Interest Company (CIC), (Spin Out, Step Up, Social Enterprise UK June 2013), which is flexible, while demonstrating a commitment to nonprofit values. In the United States the B Corporation structure appears to be the norm for social enterprise. However in both countries registered charity status has enormous tax advantages.

Payment of Trustees

As the U.S. Internal Revenue Service states "Charities should generally not compensate persons for service on the board of directors except to reimburse direct expenses of such service." Board members, like any other volunteers, may deduct expenses they incur in connection with their volunteer service, including mileage to travel to meetings using their own car.[2]

A small number of (UK) charities are allowed to pay their trustees—they can only do so because it's allowed by their governing document, by the UK Charity Commission or by the courts with specific rules to be followed. The larger UK housing associations now pay a stipend to their nonexecutive directors and this was also introduced in 2013 by Turning Point, a UK nonprofit organization providing health and social care for almost 50 years.

Organization and Management

Legal Requirements

It is a legal requirement to appoint directors when you set up a company, such as a nonprofit organization and they must be registered with the appropriate regulator. These directors then have a range of legal obligations and "must take into account a range of wider 'environmental' factors that are considered to characterize responsible corporate behavior in the 21st century" (Davies 2006).

These requirements, both legal and good practice, may not be familiar to those who have not established new companies or organizations previously. While some are spelt out explicitly (for example, accounts' requirements), others are common sense requirements (for example, insurance), which will cover the organization in case of problems. The full list includes:

---

[2] https://councilofnonprofits.org/tools-resources/can-board-members-be-paid#sthash.75x0ei9u.dpuf

- The need to prepare and file annual accounts and, where legally required, having these audited
- The holding of annual general meetings for company members
- Registration and submission of tax returns if required
- Compliance with any data protection or privacy laws
- The keeping of company books, including registers and minutes of meetings
- The taking out of insurances, including employers' liability, public liability, directors' liability and buildings' insurance
- Risk assessment and allocation of responsibility and overseeing implementation of health and safety, including client and staff safety
- Drawing up of policies, quality standards, inspection, complaints, anticorruption, whistleblowing, equality and diversity
- Staff conditions and HR requirements (covered in Chapter 12)
- Pay and pensions policy for staff
- Financial procedures and probity
- Business planning (covered in Chapter 5)

Board and Management Responsibilities

The board of directors (or trustees) has extensive financial, legal, regulatory and good practice obligations. As detailed working-up of policies and careful implementation are required, any management team will do most of this work, with numerous templates and examples of good practice available. However if the nonprofit is of any size or bidding for contracts, policies will be vetted by funders and commissioners so the board should agree the most crucial policies, ensuring they are all of an acceptable standard; the board may even have more specialist knowledge and experience than management in some specific areas.

In general boards should be responsible for strategy and policy while senior management should be left to concentrate on day-to-day management. Although major decisions and expenditure need to be properly scrutinized by boards, they should not interfere too much and become involved in micro management. Whatever the size and scope, it is essential to differentiate between roles and to separate governance issues and management or operational issues. Table 2.2 is derived mainly from the "Governance of Social Enterprises" (Schwab Foundation 2016), which outlines key differences between the roles of board and senior management.

Table 2.2 Roles and responsibilities

Board	Senior management
Agrees financial plans and budgets	Draws up draft financial plans and budgets
Oversees management	Manages operations and organization
Agrees strategy, mission, and vision	Works toward strategy, mission, and vision
Approves contracts above agreed level	Seeks out and negotiates contracts

Case Study: Board Responsibilities

In the 1990s a number of tiny medical charities were founded by rich business men who wanted to find cures for specific medical conditions suffered by family members; in several of these charities the founding chairmen kept meddling in day-to-day management issues rather than taking the long view and supporting their appointed chief executive to concentrate on the work. This made life very difficult indeed for the chief executives in these charities and diminished their effectiveness. The lesson was the board should set the overall direction and policy, while allowing managers to manage.

The Board

The board is required to determine the future of the organization, to ensure that the nonprofit organization achieves its social aims and financial solvency. It needs to set the overall strategy, goals and targets of the organization, while making sure that the social aims are being measured and demonstrated by measurable social impacts. The memorandum and articles of association used to set up the nonprofit organization should define how the board is run; in some cases, legal advice will be required to check any structures are both legal and compliant with the regulations specific to the structure.

The board will also be held accountable if there is evidence of: inspection failures, financial mismanagement, disregard for legislation, including current health and safety, employment or equal opportunities or abuse of stakeholders' trust. So this requires a board to be active and properly informed, with relevant expertise, having been carefully selected and inducted into the organization's services and operations.

Cooperative Boards

Cooperatives are owned by their staff. Some concern has been expressed about the availability of suitable board members for cooperatives and mutuals. However as one consultant pointed out member-led organizations like cooperatives and mutuals have an advantage, in that they have a pool of members from which to recruit new board members, although "proper structures need to be in place.......by having structures which involve members in the life of the business at a range of levels so that there is a ladder up and a ladder down" (Hollings 2013).

Legal Implications for Board Members

Everyone on the board, both directors and management, should be aware of their legal position from the beginning. Directors have more legal responsibilities than management: they are required by law to apply skill and care in exercising their duty to the company and are subject to fiduciary duties. If they are in breach of their duties or act improperly, they can be barred from holding directorships and if a company becomes insolvent, or bankrupt, legislation imposes various duties and responsibilities on directors that could involve personal liability and criminal prosecution. Managers on the other hand should be aware that, legally, they can be dismissed by the directors.

Board Support and Oversight

As the Schwab Foundation (Schwab Foundation 2016) points out, boards serve two primary responsibilities: support and oversight. While these could be seen these as exclusive or even in conflict, in fact they can complement each other, particularly in a small, new organization or a well-established but high-performing organization. A task which requires both support and oversight is the approval of key management decisions; this process ensures that the overall mission of the organization is being followed and, at the same time, provides legitimization for these decisions.

Topics that require board approval include the following:

- Decisions related to agreeing the annual budget, major new spending and investment
- Changes in ownership structure
- Remuneration of the chief executive and the management team
- Succession of the chief executive and the management team
- Decisions about overall strategy and performance

Boards should define and list which matters require their approval to ensure proper oversight is understood and followed. But the board should not micromanage the management team. For example, board approval should only be required for spending and investments above an agreed threshold, while management should be permitted to spend up to that limit.

Table 2.3 (Kreutzer and Jacobs 2011) defines the spectrum between support and control.

Table 2.3 Spectrum between support and control on boards

High Oversight	*Board as inspector-oversees management*	*Holistic and responsible board*
Low Oversight	*Apathetic board--ineffective*	*Board as consultant--collaboration with management*
	Low Support	**High Support**

Stakeholders

A stakeholder is a person or organization with a legitimate interest in what the nonprofit organization does, including service users, staff, volunteers, and any organization or person with a financial interest in the organization. This could include funders or local authorities who have provided support or startup funding.

According to Peter Drucker (Drucker 1990), stakeholders play a much more important role within voluntary and community organizations. So the views of stakeholders must be collected and considered more extensively in nonprofit organizations than in normal profit-making companies. Nonprofit organizations may operate in a slightly less formal manner than private companies, but some nonprofit organizations will formalize their relationship with stakeholders by setting up extensive and formalized consultation structures, including having clients or former clients on their boards.

Responsibilities and Membership of the Board

It is essential to have a board of directors that is "fit for purpose," with the ability to lead and oversee management in a complex environment, matching financial realities with the organization's social and environmental values and mission.

Choosing the right mix of experience and skills for your board increases the organizations' chances of success and survival. Venture Navigator, a business support organization, produced a guide setting up nonprofit organization boards, which makes a key point:

> Theoretical models of governance often assume that governance is entirely separate from management. However, organizations can only separate these two functions if they reach a certain size. In a very small organization, such as a small, creative nonprofit organization with few staff, the board may do everything. They may have to act as board members, staff members and bookkeepers.

Clearly the requirements for the board composition depend on the size of the venture, the services being offered and any backing agencies, who may require board representation in return for funding at a significant level. If the turnover of organization is small, then substantial financial knowledge is not essential at the start.

As a nonprofit organization grows and changes, the board's composition should also change to meet changing circumstances and demands.

Case Study: Stakeholder Involvement

Another structure—the two-tier board—can tap into the valuable experience, relationships and resources of stakeholders and service users. The board of Scholarship America, for example, created what it calls its Honor Roll Trustees, a special board to which exceptional retiring directors are elected by their peers. The CEO meets with the honorary board at least once a year and taps its expertise whenever necessary. These trustees also have a single, collective seat on the main board. A McKinsey study found that if the 32 high-performing institutions whose leadership was interviewed, 7 had some form of two-tier arrangement.

http://mckinsey.com/industries/social-sector/our-insights/the-dynamic-nonprofit-board

In fact there is an argument for boards to have time-limited membership, though some expertise is in very short supply for unpaid directorships particularly financial, which is why some board members stay on for long periods. Most boards now have staff or service user representation, an example being St Mungos, the substantial UK homeless nonprofit. Successful local business people can make an invaluable contribution to the board of a nonprofit organization; if they have no experience of the nonprofit sector, they must have empathy for and an interest in the specific organization's objectives. An accountant or lawyer can also play a key role on the board.

Diversity

Lack of diversity of nonprofit board members continues to be a serious problem in both the U.S.[3,4] and the UK. A UK Government review

---

[3] http://nonprofitwithballs.com/2015/03/the-supply-and-demand-of-diversity-and-inclusion

[4] https://nonprofitquarterly.org/2015/03/04/the-face-of-nonprofit-boards-a-network-problem

criticized nonprofit boards for being predominately old, white, and middleclass (Marsh, Cabinet Office 2013), just like this author.

The U.S. Council of Non Profits has highlighted the issue and puts forward several arguments for diversity:

- When a nonprofit's board reflects the diversity of the community served, the organization will be better able to access resources in the community through connections with potential donors or collaborative partners and policy makers.
- A diverse board will improve the nonprofit's ability to respond to external influences that are changing the environment for those served and in which it is working.
- Better decision making: when a nonprofit board is facing a major decision, diverse perspectives on the board are better qualified to identify the full range of opportunities and risks.
- Boards that are not diverse risk becoming stagnant: if all the board members travel in the same social circle, identifying and cultivating new board members will be a constant challenge.[5]

Size of Board

The right size for a board varies a great deal between organizations and can be determined by a number of factors:

- Legal framework: your memorandum should detail your maximum and minimum board size.
- Stage of development and size: the larger and more developed your nonprofit organization is, the larger the board.

Boards should not be too large otherwise decision making becomes difficult, nor too small otherwise the directors may have an unfair burden of work; between three and nine directors is normally adequate.

[5] https://councilofnonprofits.org/tools-resources/diversity-nonprofit-boards

Case Study: Board Membership

The Yangon Bakehouse social enterprise was started in 2012 in Myanmar by four female entrepreneurs, all expatriates from different countries. Their idea was "that as the country began to open up, an opportunity existed for women… to become more empowered through skills training and education." It runs four cafes which cross-subzidizes a program of vocational courses, life-skills training, and apprenticeships.

The founding partners "collectively had experiences and training that covered business operations, women and child development, restaurant or food experiences and in-country understanding." Each partner has a clearly designated role, all part-time. One partner acts as director of operations, another directs the training program and quality control related to production. The third partner handles all Myanmar-related government issues, registration, taxes, licenses, while advising on staffing and other issues. A fourth partner works on the ICT, corporate relations, communications, grant applications; "she also happens to also be a wonderful baker, sending new recipes our way and training staff on new baking techniques when she is here." (2–3 times per year). Two are unpaid and two have started to receive small stipends.

As they state "Strong women make a strong community. Our apprentice program, internships and team culture places a premium on women being economically empowered, educated and active in society."

http://yangonbakehouse.com

Types of Director

Different service areas require different specialist knowledge on their board to provide the right direction: for example, sports clubs are very different from drugs prevention projects, so it would be sensible to recruit at least some directors with the necessary specialist experience and knowledge. There are organizations that will help recruit volunteer directors, such as Volunteer Match in the U.S.[6] and Reach in the UK; but if particular expertise is required it may be necessary to advertise.

The application process for board positions should be fair and transparent, with a formal person specification and a common application form, along with advertising in nonprofit organization or trustee networks. According to Trustees Unlimited, background checking is one important part of the process and it does not have to be burdensome. Small organizations can do it themselves by talking to someone, who has worked with the potential trustee in a similar position. "You can ask things like, 'Have you seen them chair a board before? What were they like? Can they manage meetings effectively? Do you have any concerns or issues?' You really need to explore these things before you offer someone a place on your board." (Joseph 2013).

A successful board is likely to include people with:

- Some prior board-level experience
- Experience of business, finance, property management, human resources, marketing, legal practice, customer service and community liaison, as required
- Experience of providing or using the services being provided
- Stakeholders and funders

Personal qualities are also important, as the Venture Navigator (2013) paper stresses, with a need for directors to be "willing to work as part of a team," be "prepared to accept responsibility for decisions made by the board," and be "patient, good humored and clear communicators."

It could be useful to have a manager from a well-run nonprofit organization who has relevant experience of viable community ventures, as well as board members with whom the managers have worked previously, who understand and trust each other's work methods.

Board Officers

It is important that the role of the board officers is clarified and delineated early on; it seems misguided that in some guides to setting-up

---

[6] https://volunteermatch.org

nonprofit organizations no mention is made of this feature. Yet the roles of chief executive and chairman are fundamentally different reflecting the difference between the board and management, listed earlier. In small noncharitable nonprofit organizations the role of chair and that of managing director are often combined. In consultancy type or creative nonprofit organizations, it is more likely that management and directors will overlap, which is permitted in the structure of a limited company or community interest company.

However as the Schwab Foundation (Schwab Foundation 2016) states "In one-tier or voluntary boards, a single person often exercises the roles of chairman and chief executive. Such a structure erodes the system of checks and balances and constrains the independence between board and management. A joint leadership structure provides a unified focus and communicates strong leadership to the external community, while splitting these two functions bears costs and administrative efforts. Thus, organizations face a trade-off between effective case monitoring (the separation of the two functions) and strong leadership. If a single person holds both positions, the board should appoint another board member to lead on any issue that requires separation of duties, such as reviewing the compensation of the chief executive."

Board Chair

The role of chairperson is crucial. They are the most senior person in the organization, they are often its public face and they are both responsible to and responsible for the board, which in turn is responsible for strategy. They may also have to take swift decisions between board meetings, usually designated chair actions, which are then reported to the board. The chair should have a good relationship with the CEO and provide ongoing support and advice on a regular one-to-one basis, acting as a critical friend, in a constructive but challenging way.

The post of chair is seen as so important that some large voluntary organizations, such as Royal British Legion Scotland, have rules about how long someone can hold this role, while at the same time having in place a structured promotion and training process; in this set-up, potential chairpersons first act as board members, then vice chairpersons before taking the chair, thus enabling candidates to be trained up for the role. At the same time, it gives both candidates and other board members time to assess their suitability for the role.

Other Officers

Most boards will have someone designated as responsible for financial oversight, the treasurer, who may convene a finance subcommittee. Finance for small nonprofit organizations has become quite complex; even small ones must now provide pensions (in the UK), along with tax and insurance, while also producing accurate accounts and returns for regulators, so the voluntary treasurer's post has become more important.

In most nonprofit organizations the role of company secretary is carried out by a senior member of staff, such as the CEO or senior finance officer, ensuring that the proper records and minutes are kept up to date and regular returns made to the statutory regulators. Organizations should also have rules about removing those directors who do not attend an agreed number of meetings, unless their expertise is seen as so valuable that they are designated as an essential advisor.

Safeguarding Responsibilities

Child abuse has become a major issue and as a result directors and trustees have very significant additional safeguarding responsibilities, in organizations delivering children's services or providing residential or day care or work with vulnerable adults. The UK Charity Commission has emphasized that the overriding duty of charity trustees in safeguarding matters is as follows:

> Charity trustees are responsible for ensuring that those benefiting from, or working with, their charity are not harmed in any way through contact with it. They have a legal duty to act prudently and this means that they must take all reasonable steps within their powers to ensure that this does not happen.[7]

---

[7] http://forms.charitycommission.gov.uk/media/90446/safeguarding_strategy.pdf

These duties include overseeing practice, arranging training, producing policies and obtaining criminal background checks for staff and volunteers in regular contact with clients. The checks themselves can take a long time to obtain. However in the U.S. the Children Bureau[8] and in the UK the NSPCC provide help with developing and implementing appropriate policies for safeguarding children.[9]

Conflicts of Interest

It is inevitable that both disagreements and conflicts of interest will arise on the board. Healthy disagreement is good, but the chair should act swiftly to deal with any damaging disagreements on the board, which can fester and seriously disrupt business. Dealing with these disagreements can be quite a demanding process, requiring a high level of skills; away days or consultancy can be ways of dealing with them.

On conflicts of interest, boards should develop policies and procedures on how to deal with potential and real conflicts of interest, which should be brought into the open and shared for discussion. Potential sources of conflicts of interest include the following:

- Board members could gain financially from their board involvement (for example, if the board member has expertise that the nonprofit organization requires, such as marketing or accounting)
- Board members could gain non-financially from their board involvement (for example, if a board member is also a beneficiary of the nonprofit organization, they can influence its operations to serve their own interests)
- Board members face competing loyalties and obligations (for example, the board member serves on two nonprofit organizations competing in the same market)

[8] https://acf.hhs.gov/cb

[9] https://nspcc.org.uk/preventing-abuse/safeguarding/writing-a-safeguarding-policy/

Ways to handle conflicts of interest include:

- Board members must disclose all (potential) conflicts.
- If a person is conflicted in any decision, they should be removed from this particular decision-making process.
- Conflicts as well as any direct or indirect benefits received by board members should be disclosed in the annual reports.

Pay Ratios

Over the last few years, there has been concern in both the U.S. and the UK over what is seen as "excessive" pay for CEOs and senior staff[10] and the ratios between highest and lowest paid staff in the nonprofit sector, particularly in large charities. In 2010 the UK Prime Minister commissioned a review to consider ways of "*tackling disparities between the lowest and the highest paid in public sector organizations.*" Various newspapers carried articles on the theme in both countries.[11,12]

While clearly the ratio of top to bottom pay in the largest charities is in fact much lower than for large companies, there have been recommendations that "Adopting a clear policy on pay and pay ratios can be a valuable tool in encouraging positive perceptions. It is also a crucial tool for enabling a swift and convincing response to any hostile scrutiny of pay issues" (Equality Trust 2011).

There is growing evidence that staff are less productive in organizations with large pay differentials between top and bottom and where the perception was that pay was decided unfairly (Hutton 2011); this report recommended that public and nonprofit sector organizations should report pay ratios annually.

---

[10] https://nonprofitquarterly.org/2017/03/08/million-dollar-compensation-nonprofit-ceos

[11] http://huffingtonpost.com/2013/04/08/10-insanely-overpaid-nonp_n_3038162.html

[12] http://telegraph.co.uk/news/politics/12055422/The-charity-chiefs-paid-more-than-100000-a-year.html

Conclusion

Governance in the nonprofit sector is a hot topic, due to concerns about the misuse of funds, child abuse, mismanagement, and high pay for staff. It is clearly a crucial issue which organizations ignore at their peril; an example of its importance is how hundreds of customers at the Cooperative Bank, a UK mutual, withdrew their accounts in 2013 due to the revelations about the notorious lifestyle of the former Chair, Rev. Flowers; whereas previous more serious issues, of enormous debts and the disastrous mishandling of the takeover of another bank, were ignored by customers (Independent Nov 2013).

Research on startups identified that the key elements in success were judging "the right time and place, education and experience, working with partners…and applying better management practices….and technical know-how." All of this depends on whether the team setting up the project has the experience to make the right judgments and deliver on them, hence the need for a strong team at all levels.

Managers need to examine their ideas and plans very thoroughly and objectively before putting them into action presenting them externally. Sometimes the founder of a company is not the best person to move it onto the next phase of development, hence the need for skilled directors; clearly this was something that did not happen with the collapse of Novas Scarman (see case study) and the results were disastrous. Having a board of directors who rubber stamp everything presented to them is not good practice, even if it requires more preparation, lengthier discussion, and greater scrutiny of plans and progress. Boards which are just made up of the great and the good can often be less effective than ones drawn from committed people with skills especially when the situation becomes difficult.

Governance must be taken very seriously otherwise organizations will suffer. Sufficient time and effort must be put into recruiting, selecting, and training the right directors or trustees, with the right mix of skills and background, and into ongoing training and discussion with senior management. Proper protocols and guidance need to be worked out and published to analyze and define both board and management roles and responsibilities. Finally the whole process and membership needs to be reviewed regularly.

References and Further Reading

Charity Commission 2010 "*A Breath of Fresh Air*". https://gov.UK/government/uploads/system/uploads/attachment_data/file/284702/rs23text.pdf

Davies, J. 2006. *A Guide to Directors' Responsibilities Under the Companies Act 2006 (UK).* ACCA www.accaglobal.com/content/dam/acca/global/PDF-technical/business-law/tech-tp-cdd.pdf

Drucker, P. 1990. *Managing the Non-Profit Organization; Practices and Principles.* New York: Harper Collins.

Equality Trust 2011. www.equalitytrust.org.UK/sites/default/files/Pay%20Ratios%20and%20Income%20Inequality.pdf

Hollings, D. 2013. Director of Co-operative and Mutual Solutions Ltd (Linked In).

Independent. Nov. 2013. http://independent.co.UK/news/business/news/cooperative-bank-loses-customers-after-paul-flowers-scandal-8969515.html

Joseph, I. 2013. http://bwbllp.com/file/sunday-times-pdf-1

Kreutzer, K. and C. Jacobs. 2011. *"Balancing Control and Coaching in CSO Governance. A Paradox Perspective on Board Behavior."* Voluntas: International Journal of Voluntary and Nonprofit Organizations 22, no. 4, p. 613.

Marsh, M. 2013. *Voluntary sector Skills and Leadership Review*. Cabinet Office.

Reach; https://reachskills.org.uk/volunteers/become-trustee

Ridley Duff, R. and M. Bull. 2016. *Understanding Social Enterprise, Practice and Theory*. Thousand Oaks, CA: Sage.

Schwab Foundation 2016, "*The Governance of Social Enterprises.*" http://www3.weforum.org/docs/WEF_Governance_Social_Enterprises_2106_light.pdf

Sunday Times 2013. https://www.thetimes.co.uk/article/a-wake-up-call-to-charities-dn2g0cjs0cn

Venture Navigator 2013. This was accessed in 2013 but Venture Navigator has now been wound up.

CHAPTER 3

Business and Strategy Planning for a Nonprofit Organization

Don Macdonald

"I think the wheels have come off our business plan."

Overview

This chapter presents ideas to help draw up a realistic strategy and business plan for a nonprofit organization, providing case studies of both success and failure in the UK with lessons from these. It is based on research and also on the author's experience of writing business plans for organizations as manager or consultant, along with successful fundraising.

Introduction

"Those who don't know history are destined to repeat it" as Edmund Burke reputedly wrote. Nonprofit organizations are prone to the usual human frailties, so we must learn from the experience of nonprofit organizations, from business and from other countries.

Most researchers accept that the figure for new businesses in the UK that survive longer than five years is 1 in 5, while many nonprofit organizations still only make ends meet by fundraising for grants. So getting the strategy and business plan right for a new or existing nonprofit is essential.

Some research by Vesper (Vesper 1990) on the success and failure of new businesses "concludes that performance depends on…factors such as: the right time and place, education and experience, working with partners, starting with greater capital, and applying better management practices." Five key elements were identified in successfully starting a business venture... "the venture idea, physical resources, technical know-how in the particular line of work, personal contacts critical to the business, and sales orders from customers"…In addition the study suggests "three main ways to enter or to break into the established pattern of commercial activity…introduction of a new product of service, parallel competition not involving anything really new but employing lesser differentiation, and franchise entry." These should all be considered in the business planning process.

Writing a Business Plan for a Nonprofit Organization

The Business Plan is an essential document for any nonprofit in planning its operations and funding. It is particularly important at the start to convince any potential funders that you have a viable business and service concept, that there is an adequate market for your product or service and that this has a good chance of success. Some trusts and regulators, such as the Scottish Charity Regulator, even require one (or a similar document) if you want to register with them.

Updated every year, a business plan is also a useful tool to communicate to staff and stakeholders your ideas and vision, and any changing priorities. "Answering such questions as these will help: What do we want to accomplish through business planning? Are we prepared to make difficult decisions based on what the process discovers? Can our leadership team, planning group and board make necessary commitments and resource allocations for planning over the next four to nine months? Do we have what we need to ensure a rigorous process?" (Social Enterprise UK 2010).

When your organization has been running for several years, then your annual report and accounts will give a historic view of what you have achieved to date. The business plan and budget will give a view of future expectations. The two together serve to convince funders.

Key Elements of the Business Plan

A business plan can overlap in some areas with a fundraising strategy but it has a much wider scope.

The key elements of a nonprofit business plan are:

1. Executive Summary (summarizing everything as follows in one or two paragraphs).
2. Vision and Mission of the nonprofit organization briefly outlining the organization' strategy.
3. Why your service is beneficial and effective, perhaps using a theory of change to demonstrate this (see Chapter 8).
4. Why any contracts or trading are viable, including information about services, potential market, your competitors, market research, any contract requirements, and recent market trends that make your solution is achievable.
5. The team, managers, directors and staff, their track record.
6. The history of the organization, listing all available resources or funds and other support and resources that you have been offered.
7. The finance you will need (budgets, cash flow) and what funds are available.
8. Strategy for raising funds and other necessary resources.
9. Risk assessment and any assumptions you are making.
10. What company structure you are using?

In "Social Enterprise in Any Town" the late John Pearce (Pearce 2003) argues that while commercial businesses may manage just with a business plan, a social enterprise must have a plan demonstrating not only that its business plan is viable but also that its social aims are achievable and also compatible with the business plan. This applies to other nonprofits, so any plan should include social performance targets as well as business performance targets.

Stakeholders also require to be convinced about the social impact of organizations. "It is sometimes said that the business plan sells the excitement, opportunity, and rationale of your business idea to you and other members of your management team, potential investors and other stakeholders" (Leach and Melicher 2014). A theory of change is a tool that helps organizations map the change they want to achieve, and how they will achieve it. A completed theory of change will clarify the needs you are addressing and what you should do to meet those needs—linking these clearly to your short- and long-term outcomes, and your overall impact (see Chapter 8).

Vision and Mission

In simple terms your mission is "*what we do*"...the company purpose in one sentence...and your vision is "*why we do it and where we want to be in five years*"...in one paragraph. There are many examples online. Obviously these must fit with your bottom line—social and financial.

UK charity regulators oblige all but the smallest charities to set out their aims and key objectives. A business plan provides clarity on the outcomes an organization seeks to achieve and there are many useful guides to help this process.[1]

Stephen Covey (Covey 1989) wrote "Start with the end in mind." The UnLtd Business Planning Guide (UnLtd 2015) states "Social enterprise strategies are generally most effective when the enterprise has focused clearly on the value that it delivers to its customers and beneficiaries, and when its activities are defined narrowly towards delivering that value."

---

[1] https://bridgespan.org/insights/library/strategy-development/business-planning-for-nonprofits-what-it-is-and-wh

Case Study: Pulp Friction, a Micro Organization

There has been a growth in the setting up of much smaller nonprofit organization to offer personalized services. Micro organizations are those with six or less staff. Pulp Friction Smoothie Bar is a UK-based micro organization, launched in 2011, who work with young adults with learning disabilities to develop their social, independent, and work-readiness skills. They provide opportunities and individual support for people to run pedal-powered smoothie bars at different community events.

Jill Carter runs the organization with her daughter Jessie, who has learning disabilities. When Jessie was 17 she wanted a part-time job at the weekend like a lot of her nondisabled friends. Jill felt it was unlikely that Jessie would be able gain employment locally so together the mother and daughter started looking for something, which would interest Jessie and which could be supported by Jill.

They saw a smoothie trike at a local festival, and although Jessie cannot ride an ordinary bike they thought that she might be able to manage something that was stable. They spoke to a few of Jessie's friends and their families and in 2009 Jill supported them to put an application in to the Youth Opportunity Fund for £1,800 to buy a smoothie trike for themselves. They were successful in their bid and the Pulp Friction Smoothie Bar Project was born.

Initially Pulp Friction operated as a youth and community group recruiting nondisabled young adults to work alongside their regular members so that people began to build friendships and work as a team. Jill enrolled on a course for people interested in developing social enterprises run by a local nonprofit network. As a result and having identified viable income streams and recruited good volunteers, Jessie and Jill decided to set up Pulp Friction as a registered nonprofit company and to this day the operation continues operating smoothly (forgive the pun).

http://pulpfrictionsmoothies.org.UK

Viable Concept

The next stage of drawing up your Business Plan, is thoroughly researching the market in which you are planning to operate and being clear that there is a viable prospect for generating income for your specific service. One way of doing this properly is to answer a comprehensive list of questions, some of which are derived from a paper prepared by Santander Bank for the Guardian Voluntary Organization Exchange.

- Are you bidding for contracts from commissioners? What contracts have been agreed already and what are likely to be agreed? If so are there any issues which could affect your income? Is any payment based on outputs? Or quality of service? Can you join a consortium to bid for a contract that is too large or complex for your organization?
- If selling a product is this retail or to companies? Are you selling by single units? If so, calculation of income should total the price charged, multiplied by the volume of sales? Does this give you a surplus?
- Can you make accurate forecasts of your sales or other income? What might happen if you set a different price? Are there seasonal variations?
- What prices are being charged by your competitors? If they are lower what additional services are you offering?
- Will income be just from one contract only? If so can you diversify into other contracts to spread the risk and income source and risks? Are there any grants you can apply for or charitable fundraising you can carry out?
- If your income is from one or more block contracts, can you be sure the contract will cover ALL your costs? Have you included the right proportion of overheads?
- Have you any fundraising or grants being brought through? What amount of income are you confident of generating?

You must have adequate evidence to back up your answers, as at some stage the business plan will be questioned and scrutinized by a funder, bank manager, or whoever is funding your organization.

Financial Viability

You will need to carry out very detailed work to assess whether your organization is financially viable. You will need some startup funds and there are agencies which can provide these funds in the form of grants (trusts and foundations) or social finance loans (Social Finance, U.S.), Nonprofit Finance Fund (U.S.), Charity Bank (UK), or Triodos Bank (UK)....but only if your business plan stands up to scrutiny.

As well as appraising the financial viability and markets, you must analyze what risks exist, which risks you have some control over, what assumptions you are making and what is outside your control (see Risks section).

Income

You must think carefully about your income, particularly if it is possible to diversify into more contracts and sources to spread the risk. If you do not diversify it can lead to enormous problems. Likewise you need to be careful that any grants are not restricted too narrowly in what they can be spent on.

Expenditure

Expenditure needs to be carefully considered and managed. This comprises the total of all the costs you incur, including overheads. Staffing is likely to be the largest individual component. So you need to consider:

- How will costs vary with the level of activity or trading? Are there likely to be any economies of scale?
- How might prices change over time? (This could happen if you are negotiating long-term service contracts, so rising costs should be factored in).
- Can you negotiate any costs downwards with stakeholders (for example, rent free periods for government premises in lieu of a grant)?

- Are you sure you've taken all costs into consideration? Any hidden costs? Are you really making a surplus on your production or service delivery?
- The staff pay structure should be closely linked to performance, both of individual staff and the company, rather than just paying automatic increments regardless of how the company or individual staff perform. If staff retain conditions of service from an opt-out or merger, these must be incorporated into calculations, but convergence on conditions of service should be an aim.

Capital Requirements and Startup Costs

You must clarify what equipment or premises you need to purchase or renew to run the organization and what startup capital you will need. You will also need to be clear if you will incur any one-off costs in setting up the business; for example, legal setup costs, publicity, and launch. Adequate startup capital is needed for equipment, while enough working capital is essential to ensure that cash requirements are met (Cash flow). Some experts used to recommend that when you have completed your calculations, you should double the figure to be prudent.

In addition you should set aside funds for building maintenance and expenditure on equipment replacement, such as computers. Likewise you should try to build up adequate reserves to cover unexpected demands.

Financial Budgets

Realistic budgets are required, with all expenditure accurately costed. The budget should also calculate the income against expenditure to calculate profit and loss. This must include accurate sales or income forecasts, broken down into as many different headings as needed. This ensures that all the income received, or to be received, is set out against what it will be spent on. This will be scrutinized by potential funders so it is essential that the budget is carefully calculated and forecasts are accurate.

Income Forecast

An income forecast is an essential tool for managing an organization. It is a month-by-month prediction of the level of income or sales you expect to achieve. For existing organizations the starting point for your forecast should be last year's income. Each year is different, so you must consider any changing circumstances that could significantly affect income, such as assessing inflation and pay increases.

The forecast should cover:

- Contracts—listing those that have been agreed and those likely to be agreed.
- Other income—all funding (cash donations, sales, grants, and loans) that will come in for the period of the forecasts; any predictions must be backed up.
- Payments—all that will go out during the period.
- All known and assumed expenditures.
- Excess of receipts over payments—if it's a negative figure, put it in brackets.
- Bank balances at the start and end of the period of forecast.

Table 3.1 is a real life example of the budget of a small nonprofit organization delivering services on contract to local authorities, and bidding for new grants and contracts.

Table 3.1 Budget for a small nonprofit organization

Annual Income Jan 2013–Dec 2013		Annual Expenditure	
Education contract	3,000	Manager	24,000
Social services contract	20,000	Lead worker	20,000
School contracts	6,000	Sessional staff	2,200
New contracts—to be confirmed (tbc)	2,000	Staff training	550
Grants	4000	Miscellaneous	500
Grant from ES fund (tbc)	20,000	Nat Ins/pension	8,360
New grants (tbc)	3500	Staff travel	150

(Continued)

Table 3.1 Budget for a small nonprofit organization *(Continued)*

Annual Income Jan 2013–Dec 2013		Annual Expenditure	
		Stationery/photocopier	400
		Telephone/post	500
		Auditors	500
		IT Software and so on.	200
		Rent/rates/utilities	485
		Insurance	500
Total income	£58,500	Total expenditure	£58,345
Forecast surplus (Deficit)	£155		

Cash Flow

You must also draw up a cash flow forecast, to show what money is coming in and out and when, so there is enough for regular payments; for example, staff wages. Cash flow forecasts predict the likely flows of cash in and out of an organization and will be based on:

- Past experience (when the business has a previous trading history)
- Current and likely future economic and financial trends
- The knowledge and understanding of the managers and future plans

Cash inflows include: payment for goods or services from your customers, receipt of donations, bank loans, grants, increased loans or overdrafts, interest on saving and investments. With any contracts you must take account of any output related amounts or delays in payment.

Cash outflows include: staff wages and pensions, purchase of stock, raw materials or tools, rents and daily operating expenses, purchase of equipment and spend on computers, machinery, office furniture, loan repayments, income tax, insurance contributions, and so on. The following cash flow is calculated from the earlier budget.

A cash flow should be based on:

- Past experience (when the business has a previous trading history)
- Current and likely future economic and financial trends

- The knowledge and understanding of the managers and the future plans of the organization

The normal period of payment of bills is 30 days, but many large organizations save on their costs by stretching this out for smaller suppliers, which has major implications for cash flow.

For an established enterprise seeking new funding, historic reports, such as accounts, should be included. At some stage your accounts will need to be properly audited by qualified accountants. As time goes on you must also keep recalculating your working capital and cash flow needs, depending on expenditure, income, and inventory. An example of a cash flow is included in this chapter's appendix.

Tax Implications

You must check on any tax issues with the tax authorities and for charities involved in trading, this could impact on your net income, even if you have set up a separate company to run the trading arm.

Risk Analysis

Part of the plan must analyze and discuss the possibility of potential problems and risks to ensure adequate measures are taken to avoid these. Examples could include over estimated revenues and inability to reach planned targets or projected cash flows. These forecasts must be properly explained and planned for, an example could be how an enterprise plans to adjust to fiercer competition than originally forecasted.

According to some research (Leach and Melicher 2014) "the venture should anticipate and have a plan for handling possible risks, such as a delay in implementing new technologies, how does the venture plan to handle product availability or service delivery delays." Funders and commissioners want to be confident that the manager is aware of possible problems and risks and are capable of taking actions quickly to maintain equilibrium and momentum in the venture.

In analyzing the possible risks it is important to identify and list any assumptions you are making (for example, continued government contracts). You must also list the risks and any areas that could go wrong;

some project management gurus even state that there should never be any unforeseen risks, as your risk analysis should be so comprehensive.

The potential risks could include:

- **Market risks** (competition, slower than expected roll-out, ease of entry poses potential threat from other companies, your unique sales proposition [USP])
- **Operational risks** (service delivery, risks of work with "difficult" client group, issues over referral/attendance of customers, extent of reliance on supply or delivery chains)
- **Staffing risks** (availability of skilled workforce, pay structure, union issues, any requirements if transferring staff from another body)
- **Managerial issues** (good management and board, succession planning, stakeholder, and funder relations)
- **Financial risks** (too dependent on one large contract, banks reluctant to loan, low income from fundraising, higher interest rates, poor service contracts, risk of litigation, funder pull-out, bad debts)
- **Political risk** (changes in government policy, legislation, or procurement rules, lower support for sector, unforeseen political measures)

Risk Assessment

So after each risk has been identified, it should be assessed against different criteria;

- **Impacts.**
- **Likelihood.**
- **Measures** you have considered to mitigate these.

Some risk assessment scenarios should be written up to show potential funders that all potential situations have been thought through carefully and that solutions have been considered; you must also state what action would be taken if the worst happened, in other words a Plan B with a financial back up plan that will make the impact of any risk less great.

Case Study: Seedco's Social Enterprise Failure

Seedco is a nonprofit that provides health and social care, small business support and employment training in four U.S. states. It decided to set up a new social enterprise delivering emergency child care, aimed at welfare-to-work families in the Bronx, New York, where it operated already. This was incorporated as a separate enterprise, called Community Childcare Assistance, and $300,000 start-up funds were raised. The intention was to purchase child care from existing small providers and sell this onto private companies for the staff that needed this service.

A business plan was drawn up but it had some flaws as this venture was not core work for Seedco and required knowledge and expertise that it lacked. Despite proper marketing, families were reluctant to become involved, while too few businesses took out contracts to purchase child care, because of the limitations on hours and sick children allowed. Cash flow problems ensured and the venture was wound up after 2 years.

Afterwards Seedco carried out an evaluation, with outside experts, which stated that the venture had been too complex, it had pursued too many conflicting objectives, the project had been undercapitalized and managers should have been more "realistic rather than idealistic." Seedco continues with its other work.

http://cdn.socialtraders.com.au/app/uploads/2016/05/The-Limits-of-Social-Enterprise-A-Field-Study-Case-Analysis-.pdf

Team/Board of Directors or Advisors/Managers

The key elements of successful organization startups have been identified as judging the right time and place, education and experience, working with partners, and applying better management practice and technical know-how. All of which depends on whether the team setting up the project has the experience to make the right judgments and deliver on them, hence the need for a strong team; this must be communicated externally, hence the need for team profiles in your business plan.

Managers need to examine their ideas and plans very thoroughly and objectively before presenting them externally, hence the need for skilled directors. Sometimes the founder of an enterprise is not the best person to move it onto the next phase of development and is not challenged sufficiently; clearly this was something that did not happen with the collapse of Novas Scarman (see case study in Chapter 1) with disastrous results.

It is best to recruit directors with specialist knowledge in different areas; for example, HR or finance. The board needs to act as a critical friend, that is to provide support but in a constructive but rigorous way (see Governance chapter).

Innovation

Setting up a new company is not just about innovation; the Big Issue was a new concept to the UK but had been pioneered in the U.S. so innovation can be as much about offering a better or different service; Avis used to have a slogan "We are No 2, we try harder." Jim Collins points out that the most successful companies were not first to market with a new product: no one now uses the first spreadsheet, VisiCalc, or the first maker of laptops, Osborne (Collins 2001). However as Malcolm Heyday, former CEO of UK Charity Bank (Hayday 2013) pointed out "What may be innovative to someone may be just the implementation of the obvious to another." In other words an innovative approach may provide an opportunity to acquire a viable share of a particular market. (You will also need other support such as a marketing and sales strategy, which is dealt with in another chapter.)

We are assuming that you have covered the social objectives of your nonprofit organization in your planning. Some of the tools, such as the Theory of Change, outlined in the Evaluation chapter can be used.

Gaining Advice and Testing

Even when you have worked through the business plan template and drawn up an outline plan, it is essential to test out your ideas for your organization in discussion with trusted colleagues, acting as critical friends, and get as much advice and information as possible. Preparation, assessment, testing your ideas, and exploration are some of the key stages. My assumption is that you already know a great deal about the business area that you will operate in, but it is absolutely crucial that you talk to other specialists and organizations in your field, however long you have worked in your specialism and geographical area, to assess the opportunities, competition and risks.

Conclusion

Cynics say that running an organization is easy—all you have to do is generate more income than expenditure. So on expenditure you should adopt a lean organization strategy, with a detailed budget, keeping tight control over costs and commitments and building up reserves. On income you should create a viable funding strategy, generating income from different sources, including fundraising for grants (covered in a later chapter), along with income from trading or contracts; some people call this the four-legged chair model.

Resources for Drawing Up Your Business Plans

You can get assistance from agencies in drawing up a business plan:

U.S. National Council of Nonprofits www.councilofnonprofits.org/tools-resources/business-planning-nonprofits

UK Santander Bank and the Guardian business plan content guide; http://image.guardian.co.UK/sys-files/Guardian/documents/2012/01/31/WRITINGABUSINESSPLAN.pdf

There are specialist ones for social enterprises: Nonprofits Assistance Fund (United States) https://nonprofitsassistancefund.org/resources/item/social-enterprise-business-plan and Social Enterprise UK www.socialenterprise.org.UK/uploads/files/2012/07/start_your_social_enterprise.pdf

Resources for Specialist Support

A range of specialist associations offer help, including

- U.S. Renewal Energy Buyers' Association http://rebuyers.org and UK Renewable Energy Association www.r-e-a.net/
- INCA for community broadband: www.inca.coop
- U.S. Department of Agriculture www.nal.usda.gov/ric/guide-to-funding-resources and Plunkett Foundation for UK rural projects www.plunkett.co.UK

There are sample Business Plans on www.bplans.com/nonprofit_business_plan_templates.php, templates for budget and cash flow spread sheets are available from https://nonprofitsassistancefund.org/resources/item/cash-flow-template (U.S.) and a range of agencies including VAO (UK) on: www.vaoldham.org.uk/cas

References and Further Reading

Collins, J. 2001. *Good to Great; Why Some Companies Make the Leap—and Others Don't.* New York: William Collins.

Covey, S. 1989. *7 Habits of Highly Effective People* New York: Simon and Schuster.

Hayday, Malcolm (Former CEO of Charity Bank). 2013. personal communication to author

Leach, J., and R. Melicher. 2014. *Entrepreneurial Finance.* 5th ed. Boston, MA: Cengage learning.

Pearce, J. 2003. *Nonprofit Organization in Anytown.* Calouste Gulbenkian Foundation, London.

UnLtd Business Plan Guide. 2015. https://unltd.org.uk/portfolio/2-4-business-planning/

Vesper, K.H. 1990. New Venture Strategies. https://papers.ssrn.com/sol3/papers.cfm?abstract_id=1496217

APPENDIX

Nonprofit Sector Organization Business Plan

Guidance Notes

What People Are Looking for?

- A good idea
  - What it is
  - Why it will work
  - Why there is a demand for it
  - Who will buy it
- Someone to deliver it or make it happen
  - CEO or manager
  - Management team
  - Board of directors or trustees
- Social outputs
  - How people will be helped
  - Training or employment
  - Movement to independent living
  - Others; for example, IAG, work experience
- Financial viability
  - Budget of essential costs
  - Break even target
  - Income generation from different sources

Completing Your Business Plan

The following notes are for guidance as to what is required for each section, but are not mandatory.

1. **Executive Summary (1–2 pages)**
   - Overview of the Proposition
     - Short and sharp
   - The Key Beneficiaries and business
   - The Market and Competitive Positioning
   - The Funding Requirement and Financial Implications
   - Summary of Appendix Background and Current Position
   - The Team
2. **The Proposition (2–3 pages)**
   - Overview of the Opportunity or Business Rationale
     - What differentiates the proposition
   - Overview of the Business
     - Development proposals and delivery arrangements
     - Timescales
     - Beneficiaries and Impacts, Social Returns, or Key Outputs, including why your model works
     - Investment Requirements
     - Employment Impacts
     - Risk Analysis (impacts and likelihood) and Mitigation Measures
3. **The Market (1–2 pages)**
   - What is the organization's unique selling point?
   - Market opportunity—any data on current market for products or services and future prospects.
   - Existing competitors and position of the appendix relative to these.
   - Who will customers be?
   - Sales and marketing strategy—how will services and products be marketed and delivered to customers?
   - What are the price points and what is your justification for them?
4. **Organization Background (1–2 pages)**
   - Brief History and Key Milestones in Development
   - Current Status, Corporate Structure, and Financial Position
   - Summary of Key Operating Facilities and Headcount

- Details of Products and Services (including Analysis of contribution to revenue)
- The Team—key personnel, skills, and experience
- Governance—how will this be achieved, who are the directors or trustees?

5. **Financial Implications (2 pages)**
   - Income and Expenditure and Cash flow projections for at least 3 years—only 1 page of numbers
   - Summary of key financial assumptions
   - Overview of need for investment
     - Total investment required and what for
     - How gap in investment (if any) will be financed
6. **Social Outputs (2 pages)**
   - Social Output projections for at least 3 years—only 1 page of numbers
   - Summary of key assumptions
   - You only have to complete the output categories for services you provide or expect to provide.
7. **Implementation Plan (1 page)**
   - What are the key stages in getting your business up and running?
   - How long will each stage take?
   - What are the risk factors in achieving these stages?
8. **Organization Information**
   - Please complete to ensure that there is up to date information about your organization.

Table 3.2 Example of a cash flow for a small non profit, based on the budget in Table 3.1

Cash Flow Projection Nonprofit organization 2013													
INCOME	**Jan**	**Feb**	**Mar**	**Apr**	**May**	**Jun**	**Jul**	**Aug**	**Sep**	**Oct**	**Nov**	**Dec**	**TOTAL**
Education Contract		750			750			750			750		3,000
Soc. Serv. Contract	12,000							8,000					20,000
Other school contracts		1,500			1,500			1,500			1,500		6,000
Other contracts	334		333		333		333		333			334	2,000
Donations	1,333					1,333						1,333	4,000
Grant ES	10,000						10,000						20,000
Other Grants				3,500									3,500
Total Income	23,667	2,250	333	3,500	2,583	1,333	10,333	10,250	333	0	2,250	1,667	58,500
SPEND	**Jan**	**Feb**	**Mar**	**Apr**	**May**	**Jun**	**Jul**	**Aug**	**Sep**	**Oct**	**Nov**	**Dec**	**TOTAL**
Director	2,000	2,000	2,000	2,000	2,000	2,000	2,000	2,000	2,000	2,000	2,000	2,000	24,000
Lead mentor	1,667	1,667	1,667	1,667	1,667	1,667	1,667	1,667	1,667	1,667	1,667	1,667	20,000
Pension/health insurance	697	697	697	697	697	697	697	697	697	697	697	697	8,360
Coaching	167	167	167	167	167	167	167	167	167	167	167	167	2,000
Staff travel	13	13	13	13	13	13	13	13	13	13	13	13	150

Stationery/copying		67		67		67		67		67		67	400
Phone/post		125			125			125			125		500
Volunteer		50			50			50			50		200
Staff Volunteer Training		110		110			110			110		110	550
IT etc		50			50			50			50		200
Activities	100		100			100			100		100		500
Rent/rates/utilities	40	40	40	40	40	40	40	40	40	40	40	45	485
Auditors												500	500
Insurance	500												500
Total spend	5,183	4,985	4,683	4,760	4,808	4,750	4,693	4,875	4,683	4,760	4,908	5,260	58,345
	Jan	**Feb**	**Mar**	**Apr**	**May**	**Jun**	**Jul**	**Aug**	**Sep**	**Oct**	**Nov**	**Dec**	
Surplus/Deficit	18,484	-2,735	-4,350	-1,260	-2,225	-3,416	5,640	5,375	-4,350	-4,760	-2,658	-3,593	
Carried forward	18,484	15,749	11,390	10,139	7,914	4,498	10,138	15,513	11,163	6,403	3,745	152	

CHAPTER 4

Funding Strategy

Don Macdonald

Overview

This chapter outlines the importance of developing a specific funding strategy for a nonprofit organization: it analyzes the essentials elements, considers different sources of funding and examines their accessibility and usefulness. This is based on the author's successful fundraising experience from a range of funders and for a range of nonprofit organizations.

Why Is a Funding Strategy Important?

Adequate funds clearly are essential for the survival of any organization in changing conditions, otherwise it becomes insolvent. So a funding strategy is required encompassing different types of income-generation and fundraising, which should be designed to maximize income from each category. The objective of a funding strategy is to ensure that the organization becomes sustainable, and stays sustainable, taking account of any difficulties, an example of which would be a change in government policy, leading to a reduction in income.

U.S. Funding

The United States has the most beneficial tax regime in the Western world for charitable donations, described as "massive tax subsidies."[1] In 2013, public charities reported over $1.74 trillion in total revenues and $1.63 trillion in total expenses. Of the revenue: 21 percent came from contributions, gifts, and government grants; 42 percent came from program service revenues; 30 percent from fees and contracts with government; 7 percent came from "other" sources including dues, rental income, special event income, and gains or losses from goods sold.[2]

UK Sources of Income

Total income from all sources for all UK nonprofits is around £64 billion.[3] Income from individuals remains the nonprofit sector's main income source, providing £19.4 billion in 2013 to 2014 (44 percent of total income) via donations and purchases (NCVO). Contracts and grants from government bodies, worth £15.0 billion, generate a third of the sector's income (34 percent) from local government, central government, NHS, European Union, international governments and agencies like the UN. Income from government in the UK fell from 2009 to 2010 as

---

1 https://web.stanford.edu/group/scspi/_media/pdf/key_issues/policy_journalism.pdf

2 http://nccs.urban.org/data-statistics/quick-facts-about-nonprofits

3 file:///C:/Users/donmac25gmail.com/Downloads/SN05428%20(10).pdf

austerity cuts hit, but increased between 2012 to 2013 and 2013 to 2014. The 2013 to 2014 level is still £600 million below the peak of 2009/10. As with overall income, the growth in government income mostly occurred in organizations with an income over £100 million.

Developing a Funding Strategy

Any funding strategy needs to be properly devised and documented, giving the organization the focus and ability to plan for its future. It should outline the resources required for the organization to operate effectively and describe ways to gain funding.

You can employ a consultant or staff fundraiser to produce a strategy or attend specialist training to enable you to do this; there are also some websites with useful information (see resource list at the end of the chapter).

In the U.S. fundraising activities are regulated by state law. Many states require charitable nonprofits and any paid professional fundraising consultant to register with the state before the nonprofit solicits any donations. Many states also require nonprofits that enter into agreement to share the revenue from sales activity with another organization to file with the state to disclose that fundraising activity. In the UK fundraising legislation has been extended, with the central Fundraising Regulator[4] operational from 2017, but there will be a transition period as not all the regulations are clear.

Funding Strategy Content

Backing up any good funding strategy will be a viable service proposition and a strategy or business or strategic plan (see Business Plan chapter), while proper financial processes are also required. The strategy must describe how you plan to generate income and raise funds, timescales, who you plan to approach and how.

You should include an outline budget, calculating total income and expenditure for 2 to 3 years and the allocation of funds. It is important

[4] https://fundraisingregulator.org.uk

to prepare a budget for this time period, as this helps you develop a medium or long-term view of where the organization's funds are headed, while showing funders that you are planning ahead and you can be sustainable.

Different Categories of Income

The strategy needs to be clear where you are generating funds from, namely:

1. Fundraising; for example, donations and legacies
2. Selling goods or services to the public, with clarity about marketing and selling
3. Social finance; for example, social impact bonds
4. Contracts, tenders
5. In kind income (buildings, seconded staff, volunteers as in charity shops)
6. Crowdfunding

These sources each require different approaches and I will try to cover these separately in this chapter, but the requirements are so different for gaining contracts that this is dealt with in Chapter 5.

Fundraising Plan

A fundraising plan should be based on the overall strategy or business plan of the organization. For the plan to be viable, you must have carefully researched your field first, examining any factors or trends that could affect the overall mission and opportunities for the social organization. One example illustrates this; the change of UK government in 2010 reduced drastically the amount of funding available to train and support vulnerable unemployed people, which was such a severe reduction that several charities specializing in training, such as Red Kite, were forced to wind up completely.

Keeping abreast of new developments and opportunities in your field is essential by networking and subscribing to newsletters (see the following Resource Box) and attending conferences to find out what is and what is not available.

The next step is to identify the most likely funders and communicate with them to find out their priorities, requirements and deadlines in detail. If possible you should develop positive relationships with key staff in these funders; personal contacts can open doors; occasionally nonprofits with good links and reputation with a trust are offered first bite at bidding for funds, particularly toward the end of the financial year of when a trust has funds to dispense.

Fundraising Practice

In a small organization, the senior manager will probably have to carry out most of the fundraising themselves. It is essential that this is properly thought through and training in fundraising should also be considered. Clearly it is essential that you as manager ensure your organization's performance are high quality, and that this is endorsed by a good reputation and independent evaluation, as this helps fundraising.

Organizations should recognize that fundraising is very competitive for nonprofits in the current decade where statutory funds are being cut drastically. You need to ensure that you follow good practice in delivering your fundraising strategy and complete the following tasks:

1. Creating a case for support
2. Analyzing and planning, to identify different sources of funds
3. Structuring your fundraising work
4. Researching specific donors you plan to target
5. Creating propositions to match donors' interests
6. Writing well-thought-out bids
7. Building relationships for the long term

You should be careful to match all fundraising bids to your organization's strategy or business plan, which funders may want to examine, along with any other required background papers. You should only bid for funds which help achieve the goals set out in these papers to show consistency.

Trust Funds

Charitable trusts invariably have defined criteria for their grants (service, geographical, client groups, etc.) which they publish and circulate. These can change but you can get the most up-to-date ones directly from the trusts or download lists of relevant grant opportunities based on their specific funding criteria or priorities from websites, listed in the Resource Box; local nonprofit support organizations such as U.S. State Associations of Nonprofits[5] or UK Councils for Voluntary Action[6] also provide information.

Private Companies

Different funders require different approaches. Private company support is much less common than is often thought, possibly because when it does happen it is invariably well-publicized. U.S. companies are generous.[7] However only 23 percent of UK FTSE companies contribute 1 percent of pretax profits to charities; of the donations of more than £1 million in 2014, less than a quarter, came from corporations and they have been described as "the skinflints of charity giving."[8]

Some companies such as General Electric, Shell, General Mills, or Lloyds Bank have set up their own foundations, with some independent trustees, but others organize donations in house. Some companies tend to target their support for community projects operating in their area of work, probably to attract potential customers; thus AT&T's and BT's donations have become more technological over the last 20 years. Others try to build a good reputation in a target community. An example was when Grand Metropolitan Plc closed a whisky distillery in Scotland in the 1990s, they set up a local employment and training scheme which continues as an independent charity.[9] Some companies do commit funds to charities over the long term such as Rolls Royce supporting the

---

[5] https://councilofnonprofits.org/state-association

[6] https://navca.org.uk/members

[7] http://fortune.com/2016/06/22/fortune-500-most-charitable-companies

[8] Philip Collins, the Times, London 30.1.2.2016

[9] http://tomorrows-people.co.uk/

UK St Mungos homeless charity over years and Shell supporting Shell Livewire, the enterprise charity, for 25 years, albeit with the organization being branded with their name.

Companies often prefer donating to registered charities to gain tax relief, though they can use other budgets such as sponsorship to support nonprofits. CSR is expanding in the West. In the U.S. according to Andreason "alliances between nonprofit and for-profit organizations (have) skyrocketed. Avon, American Airlines...Ramada International Hotels & Resorts... and many other corporations have joined forces with national nonprofit institutions, such as the American Red Cross, the YMCA, the American Heart Association, and the Nature Conservancy."[10] However the commercial partners can drive hard bargains as they want to make reasonable profits from these partnerships.

Case Study

The marketing manager for a very popular set of children's books started discussions about working with a children's nonprofit on a sponsorship deal which would raise significant funds for them. The obvious candidate was the largest and most high profile nonprofit in the country. However, after initial negotiations, the marketing manager decided to work with a much smaller nonprofit, because the large nonprofit had such a long list of rigid demands to be met in full.

Some companies structure their donations so that staff vote for their favorite charities; others depend on more informal decision-making, so it is important to develop contacts with staff before approaching the company. Companies also give in kind donations, such as goods, services, staff volunteers, or secondment; funds may then follow, but it must be pointed out that the efforts of company volunteers must be properly directed and channeled. Many supermarkets and banks often have small funds for local community projects.

[10] https://hbr.org/1996/11/profits-for-nonprofits-find-a-corporate-partner

Events

Raising funding through events is common; on a local level, cake sales, fun runs, and jumble sales have a positive effect on the community, with an increased awareness a positive benefit. However hopes for raising large sums from events must be very realistic. It is no accident that events companies charge for their services, because professional expertise is required to make money out of these and there have been occasions in the author's direct experience when fundraising events lost more money than they raised.

Bank Funding

There are some banks offering microloans, social finance, and some start-up finance for social enterprises; for example, Grameen America, San Antonio-based LiftFund (U.S), California-based Opportunity Fund (U.S.), Charity Bank (UK), Venturesome (UK) UnLtd (UK), and Triodos Bank (UK). Clearly if you are taking out a loan you need to have budgeted for any interest payments.

Bank Loans

Most charities and many social enterprises are dubious about taking on loans from banks and other institutions, because of the interest payments. Commercial banks may even require assets to be put up as collateral, because by far and away the most important factor for banks is the security of any investment or lending they make. So you will be questioned stringently on this.

Many bankers and lenders use a checklist to manage credit risks called CAMPARI:

- CHARACTER. Do you have a good credit history and a sound reputation?
- ABILITY. Do you have the right experience, skills, and the right team?
- MARGIN. Can the bank foresee that you will make sufficient profits and any margin it can receive over time?

- PURPOSE. What does your organization do? What do you need funding for?
- AMOUNT. Have you made the right calculations in your business plan for how much you need? Is there any other funding?
- REPAYMENT. Can you afford any repayments? Does your cash flow stand up?
- INSURANCE. How can the bank cover any potential loss? Do you have any assets with value; for example, buildings not computers? What happens if the founder leaves?

Social Finance

Social finance is targeted at those social sector organizations that trade or sell services such as social enterprise. It can encompass loans and also Pay for Success or Social Impact Bonds, which are a financial bond, operating over a fixed period of time. Repayment to investors and service providers is made upon specified social outcomes being achieved, with auditable evidence provided; for example, signed attendance registers or job offers.

Case Study: Roca, Massachusetts

In January 2014 the State of Massachusetts agreed a 4-year contract with the nonprofit organization Roca to improve community-based provision and reduce young adult recidivism. The costs of maintaining each offender in the community was almost four times cheaper than keeping them in prison so there would be significant savings from such programs. Roca assists high-risk young men stay out of prisons, gain employment and stabilize their lives. Its programs were built on evidence-based practices capable of reducing recidivism rates by 25 to 60 percent.

According to a SSIR paper

> The break-even rate for the Massachusetts PFS is a 40 percent recidivism reduction the level at which the program savings and pay-outs will both equal $22 million. If Roca achieves a

70 percent reduction in recidivism, the pay-out will be capped at $27 million and the state will save an additional $18 million over the contract period (of four years). At that level of impact Roca will receive additional payments up to $1 million.*

Since starting in January 2014 over 500 young men have been referred to Roca. Roca's internal tracking shows that Roca's performance meets the projections: at the 2-year mark overall retention rate was 73 percent (planned: 70 percent); reduction in incarceration was almost at plan (actual: 19; planned: 17) and overall attrition was lower than expected (actual: 74; planned: 78).

http://rocainc.org/work/pay-for-success/
* https://ssir.org/up_for_debate/article/the_payoff_of_pay_for_success

Social Impact Bonds

Examples of Social Impact Bonds Projects in the UK include a London consortium of charities (St Mungos, Connexions St Martins, Thamesreach), who worked with street homeless and were paid on achievement of results at different stages—rehousing off the streets, resettlement into permanent housing, progress into work. A £900,000 bond was raised by Triodos Bank, from trusts and also from St Mungos and Thamesreach themselves, and the whole project ran smoothly.[11]

Preparing Applications

When writing fundraising applications, make sure you leave enough time for thorough proofreading and ask a colleague if possible to give it a read through. Then cover these points;

- Make sure you communicate clearly when writing or speaking.

[11] https://london.gov.uk/moderngov/documents/s48981/11_rough%20sleeping%20social%20impact%20bond.pdf

- Try to demonstrate innovation and efficient delivery.
- Show your passion and belief in your own organization.
- Be specific with what you are requesting.
- Show the viability of your project.
- Follow the funding guidelines and criteria exactly.
- Include a budget and any other papers or policies required.
- Make sure your budget includes a fair proportion of your eligible overheads (This is a process called Full Cost Recovery; more information about this in the Resource section).
- Try to think as the funder would, putting yourself in the funder's position.

Funders' Considerations

Funders want to be associated with successful and effective organizations, so demonstrate your track record and success (for example, feedback from stakeholders and beneficiaries, case studies, evaluations). They often want to fund standalone projects, which show their funding has made a difference. They invariably require exposure and publicity for their brand, while they also want to know that the organizations they fund have the capacity to survive. They want to be able to trust that your organization will deliver in an efficient way, without hassle or adverse publicity. Some trusts also prefer to give grants for capital funds as this does not commit them to longer-term funding.

Alternative Sources of Funding

Recently new online sources of funding have developed but there is still concern about some of these; peer-to-peer funding (P2P) was described by the UK *Financial Times* in July 2013 as "inherently unsafe"[12] with calls for these to be regulated.[13] However Malcolm Hayday, former UK

---

[12] https://www.ft.com/content/04d6bdce-f2ee-11e2-802f-00144feabdc0?mhq5j=e3

[13] http://standard.co.uk/business/anthony-hilton-peertopeer-is-big-enough-to-be-regulated-a3548621.html

Charity Bank CEO, commented to me that although "one or two P2P platforms have failed already, but (if) developed wisely, these are welcome instruments… (which) should make small sums more accessible at a fair and affordable rate."[14]

Online Crowdfunding

Key differences exist in online fundraising platforms. As the Council for Non Profits states

> Some platforms are tailored for creative projects, while others cater specifically to nonprofits interested in using crowdfunding to fundraise. Additionally, different platforms charge different fees: some charge more if a project doesn't reach its goal, while others don't charge a fee at all, but also don't allow the sponsoring nonprofit to collect donations unless they reach the target amount. In that case, donations are never actually collected/debited from the donor's credit card, so donors' contributions are not made, and neither the crowdfunding platform nor the nonprofit receive revenue.…All crowdfunding platforms charge a baseline processing fee, and fees vary.

In addition the U.S. laws regulating fundraising also apply to crowdfunding so a nonprofit network suggests "Charitable nonprofits have the obligation to treat crowdfunding like any other fundraising activity—which means that charitable registration most likely applies."[15]

These sites are most effective if you can link them with a publicity campaign and other work; "You'll need a clear idea of what you want to fund, great messaging to communicate your idea, a fundraising target and a timeframe in which to meet it" as an article in the UK Guardian points

---

[14] Email to author 2013

[15] www.councilofnonprofits.org/tools-resources/crowdfunding-nonprofits#sthash.msKILuWz.dpuf

out and you need to ask yourself some questions before you start.[16] Three mistakes that nonprofits make are to fail to draw up clear goals, to be shy with social media and to fail to rally supporters.[17]

Crowdfunding Websites Charges

Most sites charge a range of different commissions and fees; some sites also do not donate funds if your fundraising does not meet its targets, so preliminary preparation and fundraising work is essential. There are some websites specifically targeted at nonprofits (see the following resources).

Critical Success Factors in Fundraising

Critical success factors include:

- Familiarizing yourself adequately with the bidding guidelines of the potential donor, seeking clarification if needed.
- Being realistic, never asking for too much if you are a small organization, in particular never bidding for more than your current annual income with one funder.
- For projects, making sure that you include a fair proportion of core costs (for example, insurance, management, premises) and remembering to add inflation for your second and third years of operation.
- Demonstrating the track record of your organization by past experience, external evaluations, and staff competence including qualifications.
- Celebrating your success and the funder's support by publicizing the project to stakeholders through e-newsletters, websites, press releases, and so on.

Finally fundraising can be very hard and difficult work, particularly at this time with too many nonprofits chasing too little funding. So do persevere.

---

16 www.theguardian.com/voluntary-sector-network/2016/may/24/launching-a-crowdfunding-campaign-ask-yourself-these-five-questions-first

17 http://nonprofithub.org/fundraising/3-mistakes-nonprofits-make-crowd-funding

Fundraising Resources

In the U.S. Grantspace http://grantspace.org/about-grantspace, Bridgespan www.bridgespan.org and Grantwatch www.grantwatch.com. These can be checked for state resources. There are also specific funds for rural areas www.nal.usda.gov/ric/guide-to-funding-resources and city resources http://nyc.gov/site/nonprofits/resources/other-funding-opportunities.page.

UK NCVO fundraising resource https://knowhownonprofit.org/funding/fundraising. Funding sites exist for Scotland www.fundingscotland.com/; Wales www.wcva.org.uk/funding; Northern Ireland www.communityni.org and English regional funds (London Community Foundation www.londoncf.org.uk/ and http://communitymatters.org.uk/)

You can use professional fundraisers but need to employ the right ones; see www.institute-of-fundraising.org.uk. Full Cost Recovery is explained on the UK National Lottery website www.biglotteryfund.org.uk/funding/funding-guidance/applying-for-funding/full-cost-recovery

A review of U.S. crowdfunding sites: http://verticalresponse.com/blog/10-crowdfunding-websites-every-non-profit-should-know

1. **Rally** Start From Seed had success with this online fundraising platform. It's a user-friendly site with an appealing presentation and there's no minimum donation.
2. **HopeMob** This site boasts a community of 10,000+ members; plenty of great success stories, including the more than $5,000 raised for The Supply, a nonprofit that builds schools in Nairobi.
3. **Start Some Good** In addition to an easy-to-use platform, this site offers Crowdfunding 101, a free e-mail course for nonprofits. The site only charges fees if your campaign reaches its target.

4. **Crowdrise** One of the more organized sites, Crowdrise divides fundraising by a variety of categories like animal welfare or education and fundraising methods (like runs or events).
5. **Causes** Billing itself as the world's largest online campaigning platform, Causes currently only allows registered charity nonprofits to fundraise on its site. Campaigns can be used for petitions and to ask people to take pledges, such as Toyota's campaign to make child passenger safety a priority.
6. **Indiegogo** Campaigns set a goal. With a fixed account if you don't hit your goal, any money raised returned to the donor. With a flexible account and don't hit your goal, you keep the money raised but Indiegogo keep more. Registered charities receive discounts, but you must check.
7. **FirstGiving** With over a decade of fundraising, FirstGiving boasts some big names in the nonprofit sector, such as Habitat for Humanity, the Special Olympics and The Humane Society.
8. **RocketHub** Television network A&E now searches RocketHub for crowdfunding projects that it wants to feature in its new Project Startup. Fees vary based on whether you meet your goals.
9. **CauseVox** Allows nonprofits to easily change the look of their page without a developer, CauseVox makes it easy to embed multimedia (videos) by pasting a link. Case studies include the Autism Science Foundation and Change for Kids. It has a unique fee and pricing system as well.
10. **Razoo** This site allows nonprofits to host a Giving Day, a 24-hour online fundraising competition, where Razoo trains you to reach supporters via social media, e-mail, events, and more.

UK Nonprofit Crowdfunding Sites

BT Open Donate "is free for charities, barring the 15p/13p debit or credit card processing fee," while Givey donates more to your charity but…"you'll be charged 50p on top." Indigogo charges credit card fees at 10 percent.

www.btplc.com/mydonate
www.givey.com
www.thebiggive.org.UK
https://home.justgiving.com
https://chuffed.org
https://buzzbnk.org
www.indiegogo.com
https://about.spacehive.com/

Social Finance Funders

Grameen America (U.S.), http://grameenamerica.org/
LiftFund (U.S.), http://elpaso.liftfund.com
Opportunity Fund (U.S.), https://opportunityfund.org
Nerd Wallet (U.S.) https://nerdwallet.com/blog/small-business/top-nonprofit-microfinance-organizations-that-lend-in-U.S./
Charity Bank (UK) http://charitybank.org
Triodos Bank (UK) http://triodos.co.UK
CAF Venturesome (UK) www.cafonline.org/about-U.S./caf-venturesome
UnLtd (UK) http://unltd.org.UK
E-commerce http://nonprofitcms.org/nonprofit-e-commerce-for-fundraising and UK sites to advertise your services http://just-buy.org.UK/

Specialist Funds

Specific arts funds (UK) www.voluntaryarts.org/information-and-advice/downloads Princes Trust UK (if under 25 and starting an enterprise) www.princes-trust.org.UK/need_help/grants.aspx
U.S. Archer Fund green energy http://archerfund.org/about-U.S..html
UK Rural green energy fund
www.wrap.org.UK/content/rural-community-energy-fund

CHAPTER 5

Tendering, Procurement and Contracting

Don Macdonald

Overview

This chapter provides information and ideas about tendering, procurement and contracting, examining different methods to tackle these from the point of view of nonprofit organization managers.

Introduction

"Since at least the 1960s, and accelerating considerably beginning in the 1980s, all levels of government have depended on charitable nonprofits to deliver a broad array of services to the public through the use of contracts and grants."[1]

However government funding for nonprofit organizations is changing drastically in three ways; first, it is being cut back severely across the board because of austerity measures after the 2008 crisis; secondly, a large amount of grant funding for nonprofit organizations is being changed into contracts, often with output-related funding targets; thirdly, many more government services (including probation/parole and children's services) are being placed into independent trusts or put out to competitive tender. So if you are managing a nonprofit organization that has been reliant on government grants, you will now have to learn how to go about bidding for tenders, managing contracts and running services to meet output related targets. This requires specialist skills and knowledge as it can be a very complex and demanding process.

Nonprofit organizations come in all sizes but the majority are relatively small; only 1.2 percent of UK charities earn over £5 million with a similar situation in the United States.

It is likely that most senior managers will be heavily involved in drawing up tenders, bids and procurement. Some managers will already have the necessary tendering skills, while larger organizations will be able to employ specialist contract bidding staff. It is also extremely likely that managers will have to set up new projects which are best described as project management (covered in the Chapter 6). Managers may also have to update or turn around existing services, where markets or funding have changed or mergers have taken place, a process normally called change management (see Chapter 6). This chapter covers a multitude of tasks, in the same way that a range of very different skills are required for small nonprofit organization managers, particularly those where the senior manager has to multitask.

---

[1] www.councilofnonprofits.org/trends-policy-issues/government-grants-contracting

Commissioning and Procurement

Commissioning, purchasing and procurement overlap—in fact the words are often used interchangeably. Commissioning involves a public body assessing the needs for a service for particular clients, establishing the strategy to meet those needs, defining outcomes, and identifying the resources required to achieve the outcomes.

Purchasing or procurement follows, identifying the preferred delivery option and ensuring the works or services arrive in the right place at the right time, at the right quality, in the right quantity and at the right cost available, depending on factors such as social value (see the following).

Legal Framework

When awarding contracts for public services, public bodies in both the U.S. and UK are required to comply with certain rules; in the U.S. more of these are vested in state governments. These include:

1. Their own standing orders or financial regulations will require them to obtain a number of quotes for purchases in excess of certain amounts in order to obtain best value.
2. Rules requiring value for money to be sought, usually through competition. This may mean the lowest price, but can also allow for quality and added value considerations. This will be affected by tender scoring rules.
3. Government rules regulating the way public bodies purchase works, goods and services and require transparency, objectivity, equality of treatment of bidders and nondiscrimination.

Commissioning or Procurement Cycle

In order to gain contracts, it is essential for nonprofit organizations to comprehend the commissioning and procurement processes, to identify and understand the key stages in the commissioning and procurement cycle (see the following Procurement Cycle by Dr. Kemal Ahson 2016).

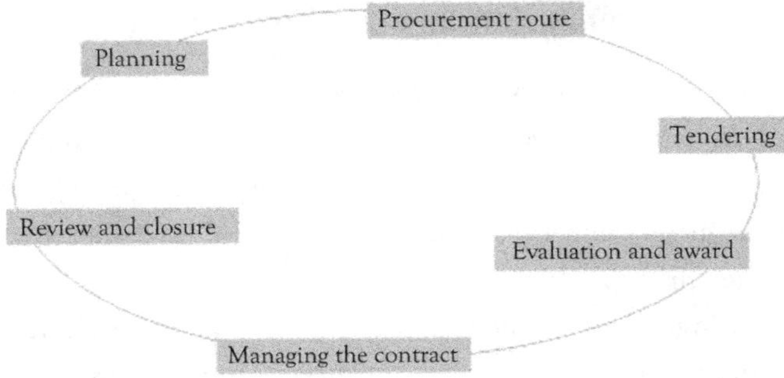

Figure 4.1 Procurement Cycle

Finding Contracts

It is then important to consider how to influence decisions and tenders positively. Clearly one of the first steps in gaining contracts is to find the right ones for which your organization should submit tenders. To do this you can get yourself on various mailing lists with U.S. or UK government agencies (lists are attached later.).

However to achieve this properly you must also network with relevant organizations, both in person and online, while you must also ensure your organization has a good public profile, ensuring there is an annual report and publications which describe your organization and carry up-to-date accounts and financial information.

Partnership

Many Government contracts are now being awarded at a minimum financial level such as £500,000. This makes it impossible for small organizations to tender on their own. Partnership is seen as something positive, encouraged by contracting authorities.[2] Consortia have been formed in the U.S. at state level (Massachusetts Early Intervention Consortium[3]) and in the UK at national level (3SC),[4] which smaller nonprofit organizations can join. Larger lead organizations often require specialist or

[2] http://public-sector.org

[3] http://maeic.net

[4] http://3sc.org

local services to be delivered as part of the larger contract and set up partner-finding systems. This is a sensible way of gaining experience for smaller organizations, without taking responsibility for all the different parts of a complex contract. However sometimes it has to be said, partnerships can result in payments being spread out over time or delayed for verification, which requires a good cash flow to survive.

Consortium Partners

To find partners, you can attend partnership meetings run by voluntary networks or make yourself known to funding agencies and local authorities, particularly officers and councilors in departments you are targeting for support.

In addition some local authorities occasionally have small sums of seed corn funding, particularly at the end of the financial year, which local councils can use to fund pilots through reputable local groups, which ensures they can gain expertise and experience. However this does depend on having a good local reputation and being known to local officers and representatives. Running pilots should also ensure that your organization is not seen as parachuting into a completely new area or service, in which your organization lacks sufficient expertise, local contacts or a track record.

Public Sector Considerations

Most contracts are in the public sector, where it is absolutely vital to research background and context. For government contracts, both central and local, political considerations, in their broadest sense, are important, whoever is in power, being aware at least of what polices and agendas are being promoted.

One director in a local authority used to tell the author that there were three types of reports—first there is the honest truth, second a fundraising application, and third a local government committee report, where you cover the council's back in all respects and avoid any potential embarrassment for all concerned. This is very much the prevailing local government ethos. As a result the prevailing high level of public scrutiny leads to numerous safety-first decisions and councils often carry on contracting with the same tried and trusted suppliers.

Recently however the pressure on public procurement from financial austerity has been to drive prices downwards and to pare contracts to the bone, with only the essentials included. Over time there have been other changes in public sector contracts, with additional requirements, financial penalties for underperformance, and risks passed to the contractor. The price can be subject to market testing or benchmarking and there can be caps on profits and liability. Some contracts have been renegotiated with nonprofits to produce lower prices without retendering.

There is no point bidding for tenders that are too large for the size of your organization; a rule of thumb is that bids will not be accepted for contract costs that are larger than your annual income and, in most cases, organizations will have better chances if they bid for much lower figures. Likewise bidding to deliver services in completely new service areas where your organization does not have expertise or a good track record is also not a sensible use of time.

Competing for Tenders

To be competitive in bidding in this environment, it is important to be experienced in writing tender bids, unless you are lucky enough to work for a nonprofit organization large enough to employ bid writers. In addition nonprofit organizations must take the following steps in order to compete for tenders; they must provide convincing evidence of their track record and ability to provide the specific services being tendered to the right quality; they must be able to deliver both with regard to numbers and timings, providing detailed delivery plans, operational models and competitive costings. No razzmatazz will be enough if the purchaser does not believe you can deliver what is being tendered.

Demonstrating Quality

As stated already, in order to gain tenders, nonprofit organizations must demonstrate clearly that they can deliver the quality of service required by the commissioning agency; this can be demonstrated by:

- Your organization's track record, with achievements and outputs properly recorded.
- A full range of policies (HR, equality and diversity, health and safety, safeguarding for children and vulnerable adults etc.), must be set up and regularly updated.
- Quality systems in place, including staff training, client feedback systems and client complaints.
- Organizational accreditation (see Evaluation chapter) and vocational accreditation if your organization is bidding to deliver training or construction training (such as health and safety accreditation).
- The experience, qualifications, and quality of your staff team, including managers and team leaders.
- Risk management plan.

There are advantages to being a nonprofit and these must be exploited to the full.[5]

Case Study

Neighbourhood Midwives was set up in London, UK, by a group of midwives as an independent social enterprise to provide a smaller and consistent service, where a woman receives all of her care from one midwife and her practice partner. However to demonstrate their clinical quality they had to supervise an agreed number of home deliveries. After discussing this, they decided to offer this first as a private service to clients, as this generated income for other potential mothers, who could not afford a private service. At the same time, this would also help achieve the requisite number and quality of home deliveries to become accredited. They went ahead with this, everything proceeded smoothly, they now provide approved services according to plan and have gone from strength to strength.

http://neighbourhoodmidwives.org.UK

[5] http://nonprofithub.org/human-resources/nonprofits-guide-negotiating-contracts-reduce-business-costs

Social Impact

Next there is the need to demonstrate the added value and the social impact that will be produced by your provision, which is particularly relevant for nonprofit organizations. There must be clarity about how this will be measured and reported through some agreed social impact assessment or social return on investment, derived from reputable sources and based on agreed outcomes (for example, jobs, volunteer positions, training courses completed, rehousing, lower substance abuse, reduced offending etc.). Nonprofit organizations must support their case with evidence, information, and case studies; it can be worthwhile to produce an independent evaluation (more in the Evaluation chapter).

Local Conditions

As already stated it is best not to parachute blindly into a new area but to carry out detailed research and homework into the local situation and circumstances. Likewise it is vital to adapt and customize the service you are proposing to the local conditions and to the needs of the customers and local stakeholders. There will often be resistance to large outside organizations, even charities, parachuting into new areas and hoovering up new contracts, so make sure the name and reputation of the nonprofit organization is known locally through networking. Clearly on occasions the arrival of a new efficient organization coming in as a "new broom" can be a benefit; I can think of one nonprofit, which is losing existing contracts in its main catchment area, because of high costs and a tired image, yet in other parts of the country, the same organization is picking up new contracts as the fresh outsider.

If you get through the initial tender phases and detailed discussions are started on the contract, then it is essential that organizations keep to any commitments that have been made and provide services as laid out in the contract. Obviously it is best to under promise and over deliver. The case study about Roca's Pay for Success project in Massachusetts in the social finance section illustrates how to do this in more detail.

Costs

Costs and income must be tightly calculated as part of the tender, with accurate forecasts for the years of the contract; there is no point gaining a contract on which your organization loses money to deliver. In addition taking over existing contracts invariably involves taking on some or all of existing staff teams which can be onerous. One enormous issue is taking on staff pension responsibilities; this issue is one reason why contracting-out services to social enterprises has moved so slowly in the UK National Health Service.

Case Study

A small UK charity in inner city London for vulnerable people, ran a night shelter and day center, with an existing kitchen for these services. It then decided to start a social enterprise running a meals delivery service for housebound elders and other vulnerable people on a contract with the local council. This was worth £300,000 per annum, a figure which had been sharply reduced from the previous privately run contract. There was an ongoing tension between managing costs and maintaining standards: food quality and transport to name two elements. The manager reckoned the charity had to spend 30 percent more than they received to provide what they considered a satisfactory service for the 100 vulnerable clients. In fact this became so costly that the charity had to give this contract up, even though it still maintains a more economical catering service for its center users. Subsequently they have obtained other more manageable contracts from the health service.

Private Sector

Most contracts that nonprofit organizations gain are procured from the public sector. However there appears to be a trend for private companies to include a nonprofit organization as contractors on projects as part of their corporate social responsibility policy. Wates, a UK construction company, spent £4.2 million with 30 social enterprises between 2010 and 2013. However according to the Wates CEO, the biggest challenge was identifying and engaging with them, as "Social enterprises tend to be small, and are often new and don't have the systems, rigor or discipline [to work with large companies]." Wates state that their vision is to work with one social enterprise supplier on every live construction project to deliver services, skills, or goods, in order to create employment and training opportunities for the long-term unemployed. They require social enterprises to have suitable accreditation such as EXOR and in turn they publicize a list of approved social enterprise partners.

However some private sector companies have been criticized for just including charities as "bid candy" in tenders to show they are utilizing community groups, when most of the income goes to the big operators when the contracts are actually delivered; see St Mungos' and other nonprofits' experience of the UK Government Work Program for unemployed people.[6]

Legislation and Regulation

In the 21st century as part of a push for a leaner public sector,[7] UK governments have tried to promote social enterprise, against the background of enormous cuts in public expenditure. The UK Public Services (Social Value) Act 2012 aimed to strengthen the nonprofit sector and make the concept of "*social value*" more relevant and important in the placement of contracts. So it is now a legal obligation for local government, the health service and other public bodies to consider the social good offered by bidders during the procurement process, alongside price and quality. Some councils have taken this very seriously[8] but there has been criticism from Social Enterprise UK that the Act lacks teeth and is not being strongly implemented.

Right to Request

In 2008, the UK Department of Health issued the Right to Request scheme, designed to enable staff to spin out of the NHS and set up as

---

6 www.civilsociety.co.uk/news/st-mungo-s-withdraws-from-work-program.html

7 http://icnl.org/research/journal/vol1iss4/art_2.htm

8 https://croydon.gov.uk/sites/default/files/articles/downloads/socialvalue.pdf

social enterprises, followed by the Right to Provide scheme in 2011. As a result more than 25,000 staff were spun out and over 40 social enterprises established. However results in general appear to have been disappointing because of price squeezes and competition from private companies such as SERCO, although there are notable success stories such as Neighbourhood Midwives, Bromley Health Care, and Devon Doctors.

The UK government created a number of start-up funds (Listed in the Business Plan chapter) and a number of support services for the social enterprise sector, as have regional development agencies and the sector itself (see Resources Appendix).

Supply Chain Management

Supply chain management is very important in the business sector. However for two reasons this aspect is less prominent in nonprofit organizations than in mainstream business; first the scale of the market is so much smaller; second the majority of nonprofit organizations provide people-based services.

A great deal has been achieved in developing ethical and sustainable supply chains with respect to Fair Trade enterprises such as Café Direct. Likewise some nonprofits have set up their own buying consortium to purchase stationery, energy, and other supplies, although these may be restricted to nonprofits of a minimum size.

Resources

Some nonprofits have created consortia to make purchases at reduced cost to nonprofit partners in the U.S. http://providers.org/business or use similar organizations in the UK www.espo.org/What-We-Do/For-Charities.

Conclusion

All these topics are weighty subjects in their own right, let alone trying to cover all of them in one chapter, so this is really just skimming the surface. However the work outlined here is absolutely critical to the survival of nonprofit organizations to enable them to become positive partners in consortia bidding for services, to bid successfully for contracts and to deliver the contracted services to the requisite quality level. It is essential to link with nonprofit networks subsequently outlined.

Simple Do's and Don'ts of Tendering

- Do put time into keeping informed about possible contracts and networking with colleagues and government, and also join nonprofit networks.
- Build up your services slowly but surely; even mergers can cause problems.
- Do not waste your time bidding for contracts that you have no chance of gaining, because you lack the expertise, track record, or financial backing.
- Check out who has held the contract previously and, if possible, talk to them about their experiences, and find if they are bidding again.
- Find out who else is bidding; clearly if there are large numbers of strong competitors, your chances will be reduced severely.
- Make sure that you have not agreed to deliver something your organization can not achieve; an example might be that your organization contracts to recruit and find work for large numbers of a target group, such as offenders, when you lack the right links, referral structures or expertise to recruit them, train them or place them in jobs.
- Do join partnerships, but make sure you are not being used just as bid candy by large organizations, particularly private sector ones, who want to allocate you the hardest to achieve parts of any contract.

Contract Support and Sources

Get as much free information as possible, U.S., https://venable.com/federal-grant-and-contract-news-for-nonprofits--april-2017-04-28-2017/ and UK https://knowhownonprofit.org/funding/commissioning

Get yourself on contract mailing lists and support programs including those for U.S. small businesses; https://sba.gov/contracting/government-contracting-programs/hubzone-program and http://www.governmentbids.com_and UK Central Government www.gov.UK/contracts-finder

Local and state governments also have their own contract mailing lists.

Support Agencies

Various agencies offer assistance, including the U.S., http://wildwomanfundraising.com/nonprofit-government-contracts and Massachusetts Government http://mass.gov/anf/budget-taxes-and-procurement/oversight-agencies/osd/non-profit-purchasing-programs.html and UK http://cirruspurchasing.co.UK/CoSE%20Toolkit.pdf and UK government support for tendering www.gov.UK/tendering-for-public-sector-contracts

Guides have been produced for the U.S. by the Urban Institute http://urban.org/sites/default/files/publication/23671/412832-Federal-Government-Contracts-and-Grants-for-Nonprofits.PDF and for the UK by the NCVO https://knowhownonprofit.org/funding/commissioning/procurement/tendering-strategy

CHAPTER 6

Contract and Project Management

Don Macdonald

Overview

This chapter covers the essential elements of contract and project management, examining SMART objectives, describing both good practice and mistakes to avoid and covers contract management.

Introduction

Project management can now be studied as a subject on its own for an MSc, so this chapter can only be viewed as a superficial introduction to the topic. Projects can range from massive new building projects, to improving administrative procedures or opening a new center. Nonprofit organization projects are likely to be much smaller. In fact we probably all have experience of managing projects from the very beginning of one kind or another, namely projects such as organizing events, moving a team to a new location, or commissioning new buildings. However this work may not have actually been called project management.

The definition of projects in project management terms, is that they are not the "normal, repetitive" activities or services in an organization, but a one-off piece of work to develop a new service, product, or building, so requiring specific and explicit objectives. They are time limited, with a definite beginning and end, so the project management team is only temporary. Specific resources are assigned to achieve the objectives, which can be new or existing. Invariably project management involves new and sometimes unknown tasks and knowledge, requiring additional specialists to be recruited onto the team or outside consultants contracted; in other words it usually involves bringing together people, who have not worked together before, in a change to their working life.

Managing a large organization has been compared to conducting an orchestra, but every orchestra member plays from the same music sheet, they already possess adequate skills, and rehearsal time is built in. However in a large project, you may have people in your team that you don't normally line manage, you don't know their capabilities, while the time available is usually limited and other demands are directed at the project management team. So this gives great scope for errors.

Change Management

Change management is absolutely crucial if an organization is going to adapt to new circumstances and develop new work methods or new income streams. "You can't change a (organizational) culture in three months," states Andre Spicer of Cass Business School (Spicer 2013). "The only times that might be possible is if there's a severe external threat or emergency." More ambitious and far-reaching organizational changes, such as restructuring, require good planning, stamina and patience, along with a clear strategy. Mergers with other organizations can be problematic and demanding, and often do not yield the planned benefits for many years. Getting staff to buy into and support planned change is absolutely essential and staff engagement is dealt with in the Human Resource

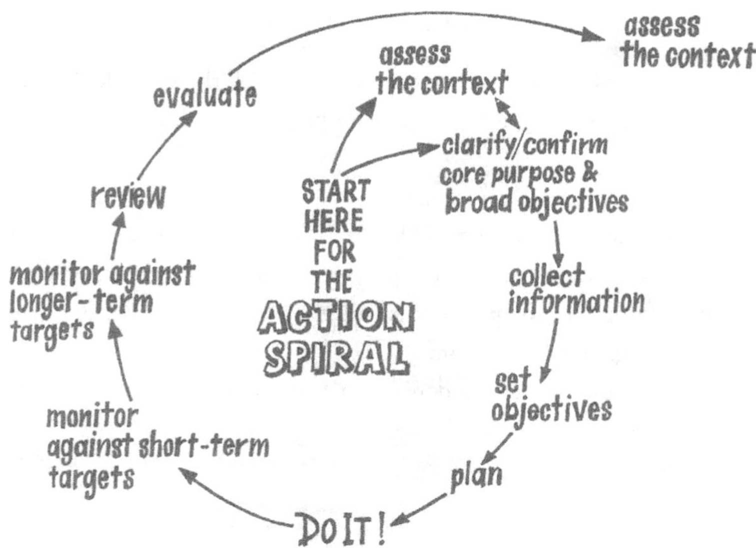

Figure 5.1 Action Spiral (Adirondack 2015)

Management chapter. It is important to devise strategies to encourage change and one way to work these out is to go through a planning process such as the one outlined in the preceding Figure 5.1.

Project Stages

It is generally accepted that there are four stages of project management:

1. Scoping the concept
2. Planning
3. Implementing
4. Evaluating the results

Before the project starts however, the project leader must be agreed, along with the main project sponsor or customer and which stakeholders must be consulted, as nonprofit stakeholders have more power. This process should be carried out very thoroughly. If this is not properly agreed and written down, others will try to push forward their own ideas for the project, after the project management team has started its work.

Scoping the Project

The objectives of this first stage is to ensure that all the possible demands and issues are properly discussed, examined, and included in the final plan. It covers:

1. Discussing and agreeing the key objectives of the project, the time scales, and resources with the project sponsor and stakeholders.
2. Identifying how the project fits with the vision, objectives, and plans of the organization or team.
3. Carrying out background research into all possibilities, including any viable alternatives.
4. Conducting a Strengths, Weaknesses, Opportunities, Threats (SWOT) analysis on the project to check on its viability.

Useful questions for the scoping exercise include:

- **Why?**—What is the problem or value proposition addressed by the project? Why is it being pursued?
- **What?**—What are the major products/deliverables? What actual work will be carried out on the project?
- **Who?**—Who will be involved and what will be their responsibilities within the project? How will they be organized?
- **When?**—What is the project timeline and when will milestones be completed?

If the scoping is not done thoroughly, problems can ensue; for example, computers installed in the wrong places in a new building. Reputed examples of poor scoping include building hospital doors that are too narrow for trolleys.

Planning

Now comes the detailed work:

1. Developing a realistic and thorough plan, outlining relevant staff, including specialists, covering objectives, work breakdown, costs,

timescales, monitoring, standards, and controls—making sure any objectives are **SMART** ones.

- **S**pecific...clear meaning
- **M**easurable...know when its achieved
- **A**chievable...so it can be successful
- **R**ealistic... relating to personal, team, or corporate goals
- **T**ime based...we know the timescales and they are relevant to the activity

2. Discussing, amending and agreeing the project management plan with the overall sponsor and key stakeholders.
3. Agreeing and briefing the project team on roles and responsibilities.
4. Identifying risks and potential risks and ways to manage these.

Risks

Complacency is dangerous. If something can go wrong, it will go wrong, so risk analysis and good planning are vital to avoid problems. Likewise it is wise to double the time estimated for critical tasks due to unforeseen issues, such as delays in building work. Projects are more likely to fail because activities were not planned than they were planned badly. Everything needs to be double checked: there is the example of different teams in the NASA space agency using Imperial and metric measurement and not realizing until too late that components would not fit.

Implementing the Plan

When all the planning and consultation has been thoroughly carried out, then it is time to implement the project plan; stages in this include:

1. Implementing and supervising the project plan, using management tools and techniques to monitor and review progress.
2. Communicating regularly with project sponsor, stakeholders, and team, including any specialist staff or outside contractors.
3. Identifying any necessary changes, which may need the sponsor's agreement, in writing.
4. Supporting your team and achieving the project objectives.

Typical Problems

There are some problems which are typical to project management. These include:

- **Scope creep**. It is sensible to recognize that people will want you to add new things to the project after the plan has been made. It is essential to check with the overall sponsor that this is agreed and that there are adequate resources available before proceeding.
- **Poor organization of resources**. Where team members work in different locations, communication problems can arise. There is no substitute for face-to-face meetings as they should avoid misunderstandings; this is especially critical at the start of a project.
- **Lack of role definition for team members**. The lack of definition can lead to duplication of work or tasks not being tackled at all. It is crucial to define clearly who does what and who is responsible; so minutes must be kept and circulated quickly; preferably an online group should be set up where written documents can be accessed.
- **Dependency on one person**. Staff will go sick or leave. It is desirable that team members can cover for others to ensure that the project is not dependent on one person.
- **Unclear objectives.** Unclear objectives can lead to confusion. It is essential to ensure you have agreed objectives with the sponsor of the project. If there are any material changes to the plan, you should ensure that these are agreed and the specification is altered. You can always change a plan but you must ensure that there is one.
- **Senior managers** leading the project team and pushing their own ideas too hard, meaning that innovation is restricted and everyone involved is too deferential to give feedback or point out any problems with the manager's ideas (see the following case study).

Case Study

In the 2016 U.S. presidential election, Hillary Clinton rigidly followed an outmoded election strategy. She also stayed distant from her advisers, protected by confidantes, and marginalized those out of favor. This resulted in a ramshackle campaign apparatus and so she lost the election.

"Inside Hillary Clinton's Doomed Campaign;"
—(Allen and Parnes 2017)

Other Issues

Other issues which can affect project management include:

- **Incomplete planning**; to ensure against this, it is essential to consult all relevant stakeholders and make sure that every part of a plan should be written down to avoid argument.
- **Project funding**; it is important to know who holds the purse strings as there will always be a trade-off between time and cost.
- **The goal posts move;** governments change, budgets are cut and projects get changed; but at some point you have to freeze the specification; the further a project progresses, the more expensive any changes are.

Project Planning Using IT

There are several project planning programs, the best known of which is Microsoft Project, though there are also open source versions. These all include a project scheduling program, with start and finish dates, summary elements of a project; the most common schedule program is a GANNT Chart, a bar chart that illustrates a project schedule. However these are quite complex, many staff do not know how to use them and training them up will probably take too long.

It is likely that most nonprofit organization based projects will be on a small scale and so will be more manageable, able to use simpler software, namely spreadsheets, to map out tasks, responsibilities, and time scales.

Contract Management

The hard work starts when any contract has been won. The manager must make absolutely sure the whole team fully understands all the contract requirements in detail, clarifying anything that is unclear or contentious with the contract awarding body. Next they must draw up a work plan that ensures that the service provider fulfills the terms of the contract, that the provider meets output targets, and that the team are keeping accurate records and producing reports on progress. Getting the whole team galvanized and motivated to reach targets is essential; it may require a great deal of networking and local marketing to publicize a new service, to recruit and to retain sufficient clients that meet the criteria or deliver enough programs, all to the requisite standards.

Very often there are delays in announcing the successful contractor, while very little additional time is granted for the service provider to gear up; invariably contractors are expected to be able to start delivery right away; the expectation is that your organization will have staff ready and able to begin work immediately; this may mean taking on temporary staff which can pose other problems.

Over performance on targets will not necessarily receive any additional payment, unless this has been agreed beforehand; however if a partner withdraws from a delivery consortium, their outputs can be redistributed to other partners.

Regular audits will be conducted by commissioners to check that the contracts are being properly carried out, that everything is happening to the right timescales and to the agreed quality standards. It may be that staff who are good at delivering the work are less good at completing the necessary paper work, particularly if clients or trainees are also reluctant to do this, because of poor literacy. One construction training project got over this issue by ensuring that literacy training was given to trainees at the same time as carrying out the necessary course paper work.

Some companies have been prosecuted for claiming outputs fraudulently, while numerous contractors have outputs rejected or funding deducted for incorrectly completed forms. It is worth delivering staff training on the subject of contract delivery and recording outputs, run by an outsider to back up the manager's directions. It may also be sensible to introduce a system of internal audits to check that outputs are truly being met and that proper recording is being carried out. As one commentator said "This.. (is).. a risky bidding environment, but one that rewards bidders who have integrity, openness, and commitment."

Case Studies

Green projects are expanding across the United States and UK meeting different challenges in urban and rural regions, but they are often too small to gain commercial bank support.

Sleat Community Trust (SCT), formed in 2004 on the Isle of Skye, Scotland, supports local economic, environmental and social development. Transport is essential in rural communities, public transport is restricted and the local gas station was threatened with closure, leaving the nearest one 16 miles away. In 2007, SCT purchased the gas station, setting up a shop, post office, tourist information facility, and garage business.

In 2009 at short notice the government decided to sell the local Tormore Forest, almost 1,000 acres, valued at £300,000. SCT had to draw up a business plan, demonstrate its quality standards and raise funds, including grants and donations from government agencies, trusts, individuals, and organizations, with loans of £194,000 from government agencies and Triodos, an ethical bank. Managing the mature forest sustainably is its main project; others include recycling, community broadband and bicycling.

A renewable energy subsidiary, established in 2007, supplies biomass fuel. The Trust is still not self-sustaining; a large part of its £230,000 income (2016) constituted grants, some for new projects. Seventy percent of the local population of 800 are trust members, trustees are unpaid, and there are four paid staff.

http://sleat.org.uk

Green and Sustainable Projects

Designing and implementing green and sustainable practice is also crucial and the nonprofit sector has been at the forefront of developing alternative energy supplies. However green energy suppliers have expanded rapidly, particularly in the United States, where clean energy is now as big as the pharmaceutical industry.[1]

Second Chance

Second Chance, a social enterprise in Baltimore, was founded in 2001 to develop solutions to sustainable employment and environmental issues. In 2003, a training and employment program was created to address the pressing needs of Baltimore City residents who were facing multiple challenges to employment, good wages, and progressive skills.

Today, Second Chance trains and hires unemployed individuals in deconstruction, salvage, warehousing, retail, operations, transportation, and customer service. Second Chance works with local and regional architects, builders, developers, and property owners to identify residential and commercial buildings entering the demolition phase and remove all reusable elements through deconstruction for waste diversion and resale to consumers.

Second Chance has expanded its training program to Philadelphia and Washington, anticipating opening new retail locations there. It had income of $6,286,155 (2014), of which contracts from government agencies totaled $3,405,569. It employs 27 staff and its trustees are unpaid.

http://secondchanceinc.org

---

[1] https://vox.com/energy-and-environment/2017/3/8/14847548/clean-energy-industry-booming

Summary of Advice to a New Project Leader

- Carry out "sufficient" background research before starting.
- Ensure the project objectives are clear and check exactly what outcomes are required.
- Keep everyone in the team informed, consult them and trust the skills of the team.
- Estimate the time scales and then increase them, allowing for contingencies (for example, holidays, supply shortages, decision-making delays).
- Sell the benefits of the project to anyone who can help.
- Always consider those stakeholders who will be most affected by the new project.
- Be resilient and do not give up.
- And keep your head, even if others are losing theirs...

References and Further Reading

Adirondack, S. 2015. *Just About Managing.* London, England: LVSC.

Allen, J., and Parnes, A. 2017. *Inside Hillary Clinton's Doomed Campaign.* New York: Random House.

National Archives 2012. *Public Services (Social Value) Act 2012.*
http://legislation.gov.UK/ukpga/2012/3/enacted

Spicer, Andre 2013. Cass Business School; Financial Times.
http://www.ft.com/cms/s/0/0b4aaac8-3676-11e3-8ae3-00144feab7de.html

CHAPTER 7

Managing Yourself and Your Own Resources

Don Macdonald

Overview

This chapter examines some concepts on how to manage resources in a nonprofit organization, in the role of senior manager, including staff, and how to best to manage your time, to organize support for you as the manager and your own professional development.

Managing Yourself

As the main manager in the nonprofit organization, you are the most important single resource in that organization. Therefore it is absolutely critical that you ensure that you always perform well and that you are in the best shape to withstand the challenges and tribulations required which you will face in starting your organization and sustaining its services.

In small organizations you will have to multitask, but it is not always evident what the priorities are. It can be very easy to be diverted from the most important tasks. At an early stage in an organization's life, it is almost impossible to visualize the way that it will develop and progress and how the markets and income streams will change; obviously project planning should always cover risk assessment, but almost no economist predicted the worldwide economic crash of 2008.

Support for Managers

The pressures on managers of small organizations are intense. It is essential that you are objective as possible in your decision making; the survival of the nonprofit organization depends on this. To do this most effectively, you must arrange your own support as the manager. So you may set up a coaching arrangement and join professional development or training groups; I have always believed that, as a manager, you gain very positive support from one to one coaching and benefit in a complementary from support from groups.

Coaching

It is essential that you plan ahead, that you reflect and learn from ongoing experiences and results, that you make the right decisions during crises and that you do not allow personal issues to affect your judgment. For me I found that one-to-one coaching was the best process to ensure that I engaged in this process consistently and thoroughly.

An experienced manager and coach, Sue Causton, defined coaching to me in the following way:

> Coaching allows you space to think about ongoing situations and a preferred scenario; what do I need in place of what I have now? Coaching enables you to think about the strategies you need to develop; what do I have to do to get what I need or want? And finally to move from planning into action… how do I make this all happen?

I have had two very good coaches, who were very rigorous, and we had a very productive relationship over years; they ensured that I continually reflected on my work performance and results, they regularly challenged my assumptions, they made me examine any evidence on which I based my work, they helped me plan forward strategies and they assisted me in being objective about staff performance and management; the ideas we formulated came from me and I continued to reflect and plan when the sessions ended.

It has to be said I have been offered two unsuitable or mediocre coaches, with whom I did not follow up. You should use your judgment in choosing coaches; recommendations are not enough; so trial sessions can be effective. Another way of arranging this is co-coaching, where you discuss and analyze issues with a colleague; spending half the time on their issues and half the time on yours.

Mentoring

People may seek a mentor when they are looking for someone to act as a "sounding board," or provide more direct advice on an issue or topic. The key distinction between coaching and mentoring is that a mentor usually has more knowledge or expertise in the topic that the mentee wants to access.

Coaching Resources

Coaching has expanded and there is now a great deal of training available in coaching along with accreditation. When I started youth work, the term coaching in social work and other professions was usually designated supervision. My two guides were Joan Tash, who wrote perceptively about supervision and coached me for a long time, and Josephine Klein, who trained me in group work. Their books might be hard to acquire but you can read about them here:

http://infed.org/mobi/m-joan-tash-youth-work-and-the-development-of-professional-supervision/

http://infed.org/mobi/josephine-klein-group-work-youth-work-and-exploring-english-cultures/

Ensuring Your Own Learning

It is essential to ensure your own learning is ongoing. Coaching and other learning can be depicted in a four-stage learning cycle (Kolb 1984; see Figure 7.1), in which your own performance provides a basis for reflecting on your work.

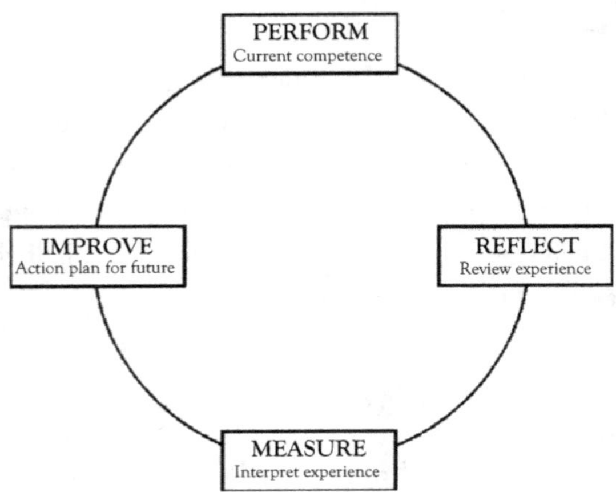

Figure 7.1 Kolb learning circle (Kolb 1984)

These reflections are then reviewed, experience is interpreted, new concepts are developed and an action plan for improvements is drawn up, where you test and experiment and in turn reflect and observe again, thereby continually improving your competence and skills. There are similarities with the quality improvement circles introduced in some companies or reflective practice groups, used in more social work oriented services.

Why Stay Informed?

Two quotations illustrate why any capable manager needs to stay informed on new developments:

- *"The illiterate of the 21st century will not be those who cannot read or write, but those who cannot learn, unlearn and relearn."*
  Alvin Toffler

- *"There is no reason for any person to have a computer in their home." CEO of Digital (International computer company) 1977*

Later on this CEO denied that he actually said those words but it summed up the attitude of the mainframe computer industry at that time, showing why they were soon pushed aside by newcomers such as Apple. It showed how the pace of industrial and technological change is getting faster and faster and requires sophisticated decision making.

Personal and Professional Development

Personal and professional development is a well-known concept, compulsory in some professions. For example, doctors and police now gain promotions through examinations. Medical professionals have to participate in and keep a log of their professional development to meet identified training needs (Luckily for him my dentist combines this with skiing holidays.). Professional development and training should suit your own priorities and personal learning styles.

It enables you:

- To acquire greater knowledge, develop better skills and better chances of promotion, as no jobs for life exist anymore and people change career paths more often.
- To join professional associations; for example, American Management Association (AMA) or Institute of Leadership and Management (UK).
- To achieve the greater emphasis placed by all organizations on agreed competences, formal staff appraisal, and professional development.
- To evaluate the requirements of your work role, career and personal work objectives.
- To assess your current knowledge, skills, and behaviors, then analyze how these reflect your work role.

Self-Reflection

One requirement for managers, who wish to improve, is that you must rigorously analyze your work, including your own specific role and performance, your own skills and strengths, while reflecting on areas where you need to improve, considering thoroughly and thinking about any relationships, outcomes or incidents at work from which you can learn. This self-reflection and self-analysis is an essential part of how you can improve as a manager. Understanding yourself is not about introspection and navel gazing, but realizing that to work well with other people, you need to know what you are good at, what you are less good at, and where you need other people to help you. Reflective practice is now generally accepted as a positive way of learning.

Psychometric tests are used by many companies to assess the type of personality you have and the type of manager you are; so it is useful to understand both the process and the results; you can do a free psychometric test[1] and reflect on this.

Most appraisals are top down, in other words carried out by your manager, occasionally involving the HR staff or consultant if there are any potential difficult or disciplinary issues. In some organizations 360-degree appraisals are carried out, involving not only your manager but also either your own staff or a colleague, friend, or manager. Arrange one of these and you could find the results quite interesting.

Planning Work

As a manager, you face demands on your time constantly from your own board or directors, from external demands (for example, service users or customers) and your own staff. You must cope with crises continually. These may be only minor ones, like having to arrange cover for other staff at short notice, or more important ones, such as giving a report to a key funder or making a presentation at short notice to a potential supporter. You will be under pressure to produce results and you need to know how you will react to different pressures. You need to know whether you work well to deadlines or do you need more time and space? Your own priorities need to be very clear, you must manage your own work and time accordingly, you must clarify the organization's priorities, and reclarify

---

[1] www.psychometricadvantage.co.uk

them when circumstances change (See the next chapter). Time management is essential (dealt with below).

Objectives

As a nonprofit organization you will have developed your overall strategic vision and ethos, with organizational objectives, after consultation with stakeholders (Business Planning chapter) and agreed this with the board (Governance chapter). As the manager you must also devise and implement practical goals for the team and communicate these to the team. Clear goals will be appropriate to the specific organization and service offered, with no room for misunderstanding the targets or conflicting with the overall objectives of the organization. The selected goals can be used to monitor progress and that standards are being met. Clearly these standards and outputs must be achievable (see Evaluation chapter).

SMART Objectives

Another way of thinking about this is through the commonly used mnemonic SMART Objectives, elaborated on in the Project Management chapter. This concept can be used to work with teams to discuss and devise objectives together rather than just being imposed, which is likely to produce both less buy-in and achievement.

Management of Time

Your time is precious and you must ensure that you manage this effectively; there are many different theories about the best way to do this. Some simple rules to follow are:

- Remember there are always choices to be made.
- Be aware what you are being asked to do at work and don't just accept anything that flies in the door.
- Define your goals and make sure they are specific, realistic, and measurable (see the aforementioned SMART objectives).
- Plan for delays.

- Start off simply for a better chance of success and build up over time.
- Prioritize your work as per the following exercise.
- Delegation—can someone do this task for you?

Urgent and Important Time Management Matrix

Stephen Covey has written several self-help books, including one with Merril and Merril (Covey, Merrill and Merrill 1994), where they outline an approach of prioritizing the most important tasks first.

	Urgent	Not Urgent
Important	1—DO NOW • emergencies, complaints and crisis issues • sensible demands from superiors or customers • planned tasks or project work now due • meetings and appointments • reports and other submissions • staff issues or needs • problem resolution, fire-fighting, fixes	2—PLAN TO DO • planning, preparation, scheduling • research, investigation, designing, testing • networking relationship building • thinking, creating, modeling, designing • systems and process development • anticipation and prevention • developing change, direction, strategy
Not Important	3—REJECT AND EXPLAIN • trivial requests from others • apparent emergencies • ad-hoc interruptions and distractions • misunderstandings appearing as complaints • pointless routines or activities • accumulated unresolved trivia • boss's whims or tantrums	4—RESIST AND CEASE • "comfort" activities, computer games, net surfing, excessive cigarette breaks • chat, gossip, social communications • daydreaming, doodling, overlong breaks • reading nonsense or irrelevant material • unnecessary adjusting equipment and so on • embellishment and overproduction

Time Management

There is a great deal more that can be considered about time management. However a few simple exercises can also make your working life more organized:

- Introduce the use of a diary or planner into your working life.
- Set yourself achievable goals by creating "To Do Lists."
- Complete a Time Audit Exercise and review this.

Coping with Stress

Stress and the physical reaction, invariably adrenaline, are part and parcel of any manager's normal life; in fact if you're in good health, adrenaline is good for you and one of the things retired managers miss. However undue stress can be debilitating, particularly if there are ongoing situations that cannot be resolved and continue to fester, affecting performance and making managers worry.

Leadership and management positions can be very lonely if you do not have people to talk to who understand the issues and also if you do not have positive interests outside work to engage the mind and body; physical effort is often a good way to forget things.

Staff Team

Your staff team are your greatest asset; in fact one mantra of management is to appoint a really good team and then support them in performing their best with as little interference as possible. Some new and inexperienced staff may need more support and direction when they start out, but this can be adjusted as they gain more experience and confidence (see Situational Leadership in Chapter 1).

However inheriting an existing team or staff can pose difficulties—they may be very stuck in a rut, producing poor performances, with sloppy habits and procedures that may have developed along with poor outcomes and standards. This situation will require skilled and consistent performance management, planning properly, choosing some easy victories to start with, repeating demands for better performance and giving feedback, in line with the overall objectives and strategy of the organization. Team work can be a really positive force. On a larger scale or with more fundamental issues, you may need to initiate a change management process (see Project Management chapter).

Team Work

Team work can be a really positive force for better performance, but this requires the leader to understand his team both as a team and as individuals. As Bernard M. Bass wrote "The leader must be able to know what followers want, when they want it, and what prevents them from getting what they want" (Bass 1985).

The leader must work hard to create a good team spirit. Regular team discussions are a healthy way of keeping staff informed, to gain feedback on new proposals, encouraging staff to inform and communicate with each other and to put forward their views. However it is essential that everyone is given an opportunity to speak and that those who talk too much or who stridently represent their own views are not allowed to dominate. Likewise the manager themselves should not talk all the time, but must give time and space for staff to express their own views; a good rule-of-thumb is "trust the group," as inevitably different team members will challenge and question each other's views.

Managing team meetings is a very skilled task; it requires the manager to have an understanding of how groups operate, to know when to talk themselves, when to keep quiet and to trust other people in the group, when to veto decisions, when to let the team make decisions, when to take action on staff performance and when to keep quiet.

Another useful precept is that group work is "talking to individuals afterwards," that is more one-to-one communication. There is a limit on the size of teams for effective group work; I believe no more than twelve staff. Of course large organizations are likely to be composed of several teams and organizational meetings (for example, all managers in an organization) are more unwieldy to organize effectively and to deliver positive results, but it is still worth attempting. Away days can be a good vehicle to tap into staff ideas as well as building up a more cohesive team spirit; team meetings are essential.

If you can build a good team spirit with a culture of trust, this increases the potential of the organization to a point where there is joint problem solving, shared ownership of the organization and collaborative working.

Case Study

A new project was set up by a charity with funding from different statutory agencies on service contracts to provide holistic provision for young offenders and young people in care, with different targets to be achieved. A mainly experienced staff team was appointed, who the manager encouraged to assist in the detailed design of the service following the objectives of the project, previously agreed with the funders. Team meetings were generally very positive, examining progress, discussing setbacks and proposing new ways forward. However one of the youngest and least experienced staff members would never volunteer for any task requested by the manager in that meeting. Yet the staffer would invariably cooperate or volunteer when asked by the manager one-to-one outside the meeting.

As Williams writes

> Those responsible for others need to be able to encourage oftentimes highly talented, committed and spirited individuals, yet have the humility, interpersonal skills and sensitivity to ensure that teams work effectively together—that the "we" of leadership dominates (not the "I"): as such it is necessary to recruit for leaders those that can facilitate; that can enable people to work to their full potential in the service of others (Williams 2007).

Conclusion

In small organizations, managers need to multitask and should be very clear about their own time priorities to make sure they concentrate on key tasks. To achieve all these requirements, managers will need to invest in their own training and coaching.

To survive organizations also need to keep learning at all levels, and then changing and adapting; the manager needs to be at the forefront of that process themselves, setting an example and encouraging others along the same route so that the organization continues to learn.

References and Further Reading

Bass, B.M. 1985. *"Leadership and Performance Beyond Expectations."* New York: Free Press.

Covey, S.R., Merrill, A.R., and Merrill R.R. (1994) *First Things First: To Live, to Love, to Learn, to Leave a Legacy.* New York: Simon and Schuster.

Kolb, D.A. 1984. *Experiential Learning: Experience as the Source of Learning and Development.* NJ: Englewood Cliffs.

Williams, I. 2007. "The Nature of Highly Effective Community and Voluntary Organizations." www.dochas.ie/pages/resources/documents/Williams_on_Effective_CVOs.pdf#page=2andzoom=auto,0,431

CHAPTER 8

Service Planning, Monitoring, Evaluating, and Improving a Nonprofit Organization

Don Macdonald and Charles Oham

Overview

This chapter covers key aspects of service planning, managing quality of service delivery within organizations, monitoring and evaluating services and initiating improvements. Various frameworks for evaluating and improving performance in a nonprofit organization, are examined, including the Triangle Outcomes Star and the Theory of Change.

Introduction

Sustaining a nonprofit organization is just as hard as starting a new one. Society and Governments change, while organizations develop and evolve, in both positive and negative ways, as they adapt to changing circumstances. A manager needs to be attentive to the internal and external changes taking place, as this has an impact on the performance of the organization. Funding variations can be both swift and substantial, causing disruption or hampering the social objectives of the organization. In addition stakeholders such as funders are demanding more evidence in terms of the social impact of an organization, service users require greater input, while many nonprofit organizations are learning and applying new models of measuring and evaluating social impact (see Case Study).

The first duty of a community organization is to survive, enabling the organization to fulfill its objectives (Drucker 1990). For this to happen it is essential that the senior manager works consistently hard to encourage a positive organizational culture, from top to bottom by getting staff and volunteers contributing to the development of the nonprofit organization and harnessing their ideas and commitment. This requires organizations to develop consistently, to monitor and evaluate their services on an ongoing basis, to plan ahead, to undergo continuous improvement and if necessary to undertake a change management program by introducing new models of work and evaluation (see St Mungos case study) but at the same time work on getting a buy-in from staff and volunteers.

Not adapting to change can have drastic consequences, such as loss of contracts, staff redundancies or even complete closure, as happens when governments change funding regimes. Adapting to change requires a good understanding of organizational culture, because knowing how things are conducted and who holds the real power in an organization enables a manager to devise and implement the right strategies for change and development.

Monitoring and Evaluating Services

Clearly any nonprofit organization delivering services should monitor on an ongoing basis that they provide good quality services with regard to numbers worked with, the right beneficiary group, the efficacy of the services provided and any progression by clients (for example, qualifications gained). Monitoring is about systematically collecting and analyzing information on the delivery of services, to examine the quality of the service delivery and answer questions about your project from funders and other agencies, for instance about value for money (NCVO). When we monitor an activity, it is accepted that we first observe this, then we measure it.

Monitoring systems should be designed and implemented from the planning phase of a nonprofit organization, although sometimes commissioners and funding agencies later impose their own monitoring requirements and targets.

A system for capturing and analyzing vital data at crucial delivery points is critical to demonstrate the effectiveness of a nonprofit organization. Specific information captured by implementing a simple monitoring information system should contain:

- Numbers and profile of users (ethnic origin, gender, age, geographic residence, background with regard to the service provided; for example, employment status for job-finding projects).
- Actual services provided to different clients, including support and meetings.
- Advice and information and signposting to other agencies provided to clients.
- Outputs and targets met (placements into work, staying in work, lower reoffending rates).
- Information (minutes of meetings, file notes, client records, records of numbers of service users).

- Feedback and self-assessment from clients (learner diaries) and from stakeholders and partner agencies (Probation or Parole, Schools, Social Services).
- Any other information relevant to the organization's work.

The channels for collecting information to use for monitoring include:

- Application forms to collect information about clients
- Registers or swipe cards to collect attendance information
- Examination and qualification returns to assess progression
- Reports from staff at critical junctures, preferably digitized for efficiency
- Specific evaluation forms for clients to provide feedback and to assess progress;
- Focus groups, learner diaries and surveys, which may be harder to collect without incentives or face-to-face collection
- Video and sound recordings, particularly from clients

Unless your organization is absolutely tiny, you will almost certainly need a computer program to record and analyze any data collected, possibly a spread sheet or a Customer Relationship Manager (CRM) database. but there are even some free ones available https://www.quora.com/What-is-the-best-open-source-CRM-for-a-small-non-profit and http://www.smallcharities.org.uk/resources-databases/

There are also certain new UK government regulations on data collection and retention, which must be followed.

Evaluation

Evaluation is the process of analyzing information and data captured through monitoring, critically examining this, then looking at ways of adding value to the service. Evaluation is effective only where an effective monitoring system is in place. A key aspect of evaluation is to make judgments about the performance of a project, or intervention and to make any necessary changes and improvements required (CES 2010).

Evaluation requires the ability to make qualitative or quantitative judgments, to set out reasoned arguments and to criticize constructively (Hussey and Hussey 1997). There must also be some form of planning along with the evaluation to design a way forward if a project is failing. Projects have often succeeded on their second attempt after an initial evaluation has taken place and adjustments made (see the following). Therefore, the objective of an evaluation process is to find out what has really happened, with the aim of measuring outcomes against targets; and, if necessary, to take corrective measures if targets are not being met.

The rationale for evaluation can be summed up as to:

- Provide information to staff and stakeholders on good practice and the effectiveness of service delivery and projects.
- Assist with lessons learnt within an organizations or assess why targets were or were not achieved.
- Inform planning and review of projects and deliverables.
- Evaluate the effectiveness of different work methods and improve service delivery and management.
- Review resource allocation in relation to outputs or services.
- Influence strategic planning and policy.

Evaluation Process

The process of evaluation should include the following stages:

- Planning
- Design of information collection method
- Data collection—primary and secondary
- Analysis and interpretation
- Dissemination and reporting to stakeholders and funders

The different elements that can be evaluated include the following:

- Outputs: Specific quantifiable objective targets that have been achieved; for example, qualifications, numbers of people trained or service users advised.

- Outcomes: Changes that come about as a result of the program. Judgments must be made of what was achieved and evidence provided to back this up; for example, if the outcome is progress into a job, the evidence is a job offer letter; if the outcome is better literacy, the evidence is an improved test score.

With some projects one may only be able to measure soft outcomes, such as increased confidence or skills, rather than hard outcomes such as job entry; evidence for improved self-confidence could come from feedback from staff or teachers. A nonprofit organization could also argue that the outcomes of a program took place on a broader level but they would still need to provide evidence; for example, feedback from residents' groups or police that a neighborhood is now safer.

Demonstrating Effectiveness

Increasingly organizations are being pressed to demonstrate and prove their effectiveness in a range of different ways. This could be by:

- Monitoring of achievement of Targets or Outputs (See above)
- Impact Measurement or Social Return on Investment (SROI) (see Case Study on REDF shown in the following)
- Performance Monitoring System; for example, Outcomes Star (see Case Study at the end)
- Value for Money
- Future need for the project

Evaluation Structure

It must be borne in mind that there are differences between the evaluation of one project and that of a whole organization. Effective organizational evaluation includes effective organizational evaluation include feedback from funders and service users. It is important to set realistic targets, though this may require strong negotiation with funders. The benefits of regular and rigorous monitoring and evaluation are to highlight good practice,

Case Study: Use of Social Return on Investment (SROI) at REDF

Roberts Enterprise Development Fund's (REDF) mission in the U.S. was to create training and job opportunities to help people move out of poverty.

Rather than distribute relatively small grants to a large number of organizations, REDF approached its mission in the manner of a venture capitalist. REDF made investments in a limited number of social purpose enterprises. These companies sold goods and services, using employees that were primarily from targeted groups that were difficult to employ, such as at-risk youth, recovering substance abusers, disabled people, homeless people and those with criminal backgrounds.

REDF measured both the economic and socioeconomic returns on its invested capital. Each portfolio company prepared SROI reports calculating the "enterprise value" and "social purpose value" of the company, which were then combined into a "blended value." The enterprise value was the financial value of the company, using traditional financial measures projected into the future with an appropriate discount rate. An enterprise index of return was calculated by dividing enterprise value by the total investment to date.

The social purpose value and return were determined in the same way as the enterprise value, except that social cost savings and revenue contributions of the socioeconomic factors were used to determine value. These included items such as increases in employee tax payments and reduction of employee dependence on public services. Much of this data was obtained through periodic interviews with employees.

Finally, a total "blended" value was determined by adding the enterprise and socioeconomic values. Each REDF portfolio company prepares an annual SROI report, which helped determine if it is achieving its mission, and identify any improvements that should be made.

Roberts Enterprise Development Fund http://redf.org
https://gsb.stanford.edu/gsb-cmis/gsb-cmis-download-auth/354066

analyze gaps in service or provision, support continuous improvement, show competence and transparency, and lead to innovation.

Continuous Improvement

Having collected information about service delivery and properly evaluated both the outcomes and work methods, the next step is to ensure continuous improvement within all parts of the organization. As Drucker stated

> One strategy is practically infallible: refocus and change the organization when you are successful.....If you don't improve it, you will go downhill pretty fast. The best rule for improvement strategies is to put your efforts into your successes. Improve the areas of success, and change them (Drucker 1990).

However this can sometimes be hard to achieve in practice. It is essential is to co-opt staff and gain their support, so this must start at the design stage and staff feedback gathered after monitoring and evaluation have started.

Managing Quality

One important ingredient in managing quality is the size of the organization; in small organizations a manager can support, supervise, and encourage staff directly, while at the same time monitoring and improving quality. However in larger organizations it becomes necessary to appoint team leaders and middle managers, even quality officers, with monitoring systems that are set up that must be evaluated and managed themselves, which gives opportunities for interdepartmental issues to rear their ugly heads. Under promise and over deliver is a very good maxim. However, there is always a need for quality monitoring systems to gain feedback from customers, to improve service delivery and to demonstrate value for money to commissioners and funders.

Another aspect to consider is whether the organization is new. Some suggest that pioneering organizations perform better, because there is a pioneering purpose uniting and motivating the team, along with time preparing and "working up" the new organization and teams. However others suggest new teams are more likely to make mistakes because they have less experience. One way of moderating inexperience is to recruit a diverse team to include those with some experience.

Case Study: Outcomes Star; Performance Measurement System

St Mungos, a UK housing charity, worked with Triangle, a social consulting company, to develop an outcomes measurement system, the Outcomes Star in 2003 (see the following Figure 8.1). With their key-workers, clients rate their own progress in ten areas of a person's life. St Mungos states this is "now the leading outcome measurement tool in the homelessness sector, and…is advocated as an example of good practice by Central Government and an increasing number of London Local Authorities." www.mungos.org.uk/effectiveness

Triangle have adapted the Outcomes Star for use with other vulnerable client groups, including young people; www.outcomesstar.org.uk/

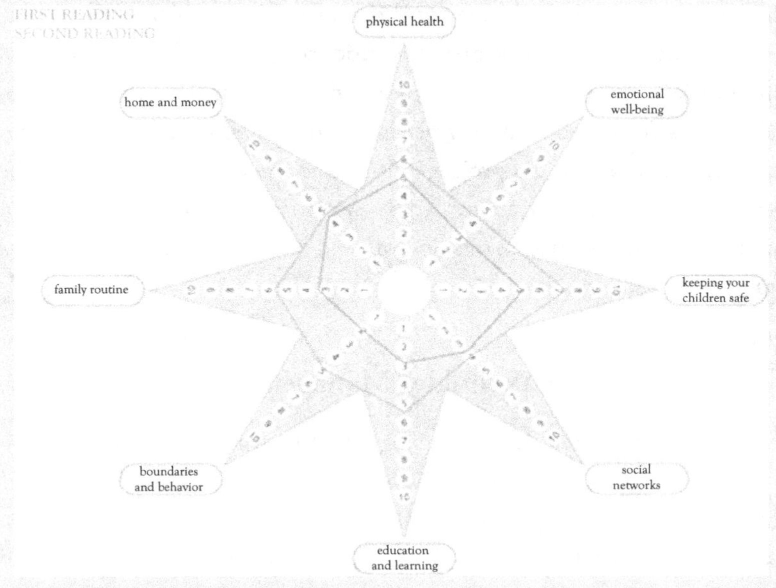

Figure 8.1 Triangle Outcomes Star

It is also important to be clear on exactly which services are being provided, what these require and what regulations are in place; if 24-hour care and accommodation are being provided for a high risk group, then many more health and safety measures are required than in organizations providing day care or training to a low risk general group.

In addition there are possible tensions over the achievement of different objectives, particularly within target-driven projects where a conflict can arise between providing quality services to fewer numbers of clients or achieving larger output numbers as required by a contract; an example was the meals on wheels project case study in the contracts chapter.

Although commissioners and procurement officers do require minimum quality levels, there can be a danger that sometimes too much time and emphasis can be placed on writing policies and completing evaluation returns rather than providing high quality services.

Delivering High Quality Levels

The first thing a new manager must do is to assess the capability, strengths, and weaknesses of their organization. To find out what is working and is not, what the prospects are for different services, which staff are performing well, which work methods produce good results, what quality, monitoring, and evaluation systems are in place. It may be that the organization is doing well and only needs fine-tuning; if it needs major management change, this is a project in itself and the quicker this is done the less painful for everyone concerned. New managers do have a honeymoon period and most organizations do not need to be as result-driven as football teams.

Stakeholder Management

Stakeholder management is a strategy used to win support in organizations, identifying the key people who have to be won over. You use the opinions of the most powerful stakeholders to shape your projects at an early stage and get them to fully understand what you are trying to do and the benefits of your project. Not only does this make it more likely that they will support you, their input can also improve the quality of your project and win more resources—making it more likely that your projects will be successful. You anticipate what people's reactions to your project may be, and build into your plan the actions that will win people's support.

The first step in stakeholder analysis is to identify who your stakeholders are. The next step is to work out their power, influence, and interest, so you know who you should focus on. The final step is to develop a good understanding of the most important stakeholders so you know how they are likely to respond, working out how to win their support—you can map this analysis. But you must make sure the strategy is based on a correct appraisal of the situation and stakeholders.

Quality Accreditation

Some government contracts require tendering organizations to demonstrate their competence through quality accreditation. Companies such as BT have even required that all their suppliers have accreditation such as ISO 9001 the from International Organization for Standardization (ISO 2015). In the U.S., B Corps are "for-profit companies certified by the nonprofit B Lab to meet rigorous standards of social and environmental performance, accountability, and transparency."[1] Accreditation for Fair Trade practice and sustainability can also be important with regard to sustainability.

The Standards for Excellence program provides an Ethics and Accountability Code for the Nonprofit Sector in the U.S. with specific benchmarks "that provide a structured approach to building capacity, accountability, and sustainability in your organization."[2] Charity Navigator rates organizations against a complex series of fiscal responsibility and transparency standards,[3] while a framework to measure social impact comes from McKinsey.[4] There are also specific UK quality systems for nonprofits including the PQASSO Quality Mark (NCVO PQASSO) as well as the Social Enterprise Quality Mark.[5]

---

1 https://bcorporation.net/what-are-b-corps/about-b-lab

2 https://standardsforexcellence.org

3 https://www.charitywatch.org

4 http://mckinseyonsociety.com/social-impact-assessment

5 https://www.socialenterprisemark.org.uk/

Theory of Change

Another way to ensure that the objectives of a project are met and monitoring and evaluation are soundly based is to use a framework known as the Theory of Change (TOC). Developed by the Aspen Institute,[6] it defines long-term goals such as the actual change that is desired and works backwards to identify critical success factors that are necessary to achieve the long-term goal. Table 8.1 shows a TOC mapping exercise, outlining the various outcomes, outputs and activities necessary to achieve the long term output. It is important that staff, volunteers and beneficiaries are involved in the developing the Theory of Change to bring a wide range of ideas and perspectives that are crucial for the success of the project.

Inspection and Standards

Effective monitoring and evaluation of services should be driven by customer and client satisfaction; with the growth of social media the influence of public opinion has become even more powerful. There are also statutory regulations and standards to be met. These can be met by systems to provide regular internal monitoring and evaluation, along with collecting feedback from customers and clients, but also there will be a need for reporting to and inspections by the requisite authorities and the results of all these can be used in any future tendering process.

Table 8.1 Theory of Change showing the mapping of an employment project

Activities	Outputs	Short-term outcomes	Medium-term outcomes	Long-term impact
Employment preparation and skills training for 300 local unemployed people	Skills training and job search attended by 300 local unemployed people	100 people going into work or self-employment and 50 going onto further education	70 percent of people still in work self-employment or further education	Greater levels of employment wealth, better health and well-being in the community

---

6 https://aspeninstitute.org/publications/theory-change-tool-strategic-planning-report-early-experiences/

Conclusion

We have considered the critical role of monitoring and evaluation in nonprofit organizations. Various models can improve the performance of nonprofits through the implementation of high standard processes of monitoring and evaluation. It makes sense to set up appropriate systems to ensure that staff work to a high standard, to examine your services regularly and rigorously and ensure that your nonprofit organization is providing high quality services, reaching the right target groups of beneficiaries and achieving social impact and value for money.

However management by numbers does not always work. It is essential to choose the right monitoring systems and avoid overburdening the staff and volunteers in your organization, of whatever size, with undue red tape and paper work. Deciding on the right tools, piloting these and training staff will help ensure the right services are delivered to the right client group, to pass inspections and make sure that the nonprofit organization is heading in the right direction. "Work smarter not harder" is an old dictum, but it still applies to nonprofit organizations trying to survive in very competitive markets.

References and Further Reading

Drucker, P. 1990. *Managing the Non-Profit Organization Practices and Principles.* New York: Harper Collins.

Hussey, J., and R. Hussey. 1997. *Business Research a Practical Guide for Undergraduate and Postgraduate Students.* London: Macmillan Business.

ISO (International Organization for Standardization). 2015. www.iso.org/iso/about

NCVO https://www.ncvo.org.uk/practical-support/quality-and-standards

NCVO PQASSO https://www.ncvo.org.uk/2-content/838-pqasso-quality-mark-the-basics#What_is_the_PQASSO_Quality_Mark

CHAPTER 9

Human Resource Management in Nonprofit Organizations

Don Macdonald

Overview

This chapter outlines theories and practice of staff management that are relevant to nonprofit organizations. It examines the use of management skills, including teamwork and coaching, recruitment, motivating and supporting directors, staff, volunteers to build a cohesive approach and progress as a nonprofit organization.

Introduction

If you go into any newsagents, you will see an endless supply of management books, recommending different solutions or styles. This illustrates the constantly changing fashions in management, in the same way Human Resources (HR) is sometimes now called Talent Management and previously was called Personnel Management. I will stick with HR and try to pick out the wheat from the chaff to produce something of value.

Charles Handy (Handy 1993) suggests there are over 60 different variables which influence good staff management, including staff skills, motivation, relationships, and structures. He suggests that "selective focusing…or… 'Reductionism'…will not do for the manager who has to put the lot together and make it work: beware the manager who hawks one patent cure."

Managing in the nonprofit sector is very different from managing in the private sector. As Peter Drucker (Drucker 1990) wrote that "CVOs (Community and Voluntary Organizations) have to deal with a greater variety of stakeholders and constituencies than the average business." He noted that one of the basic differences between for-profit and nonprofit sectors is that "CVOs (Community and Voluntary Organizations) always have a multitude of constituencies…There have always been a multitude of groups, each with a veto power."

The primary task of a nonprofit organization is not just about breaking even financially, but meeting social objectives, which then overlay and affect any financial objectives. Many nonprofit organizations cannot move forward far or fast enough together in the same direction, because not all staff and directors agree on the same objectives. In addition mergers between organizations can lead to problems, let alone any resulting changes in staff conditions of service. These can affect staff motivation in major ways, as can fear about losing jobs.

Many nonprofit organizations struggle continually to generate sufficient funds and income, which can require changes in service delivery and staffing, sometimes at short notice. In turn this places pressures on managers, who must understand teamwork and other HR and management skills, such as change management (see Chapter 8).

People management is not an exact science, research into how people behave can produce inexact results, "entrepreneurship is a young... research field" (Landström 2007). Numerous different management theories are propagated by self-help gurus, which can just confuse the average manager. In this role, you are dealing with peoples' livelihoods and aspirations, working with their personalities and your own, trying to harness a team composed of people from diverse backgrounds to work well together, toward the organization's own objectives. All these make management demanding.

Societal Changes

Several changes in particular have taken place over the last 20 years that have had a profound effect on staff management; first we have become a much more litigious society (Furedi 2012): as a result there are increasing obligations and responsibilities (both legal and nonlegal) on recruitment and treating staff fairly; this has been reinforced by increased litigation through employment tribunals and resulting publicity; second it is now accepted that the "command and control style of management are not going to work anymore" (Clarke 2013) and staff, particularly those from younger generations, expect and "like consensus and collaboration."

Nonprofit organization managers may also become caught in a values trap. Their commitment to better employment rights and conditions for workers means that they have tended to avoid some of the tougher HR practices of their commercial counterparts, such as competence testing, zero hours contracts, and performance-related pay. In some cases this commitment leaves them vulnerable to being exploited by those few staff who in reality lack the competences to do their jobs. Managers need to be objective about their staff's (and their own) performance and act accordingly in the best interests of the organization.

Another change is that all companies are now held to account by the public and media for any bad or antisocial avoidance behavior; an example being the way that Starbucks sales have gone down since being accused of tax avoidance, while Google's brand has been damaged by its tax according to newspaper reports (Daily Telegraph 2013), and charity behavior has also been under close scrutiny particularly with regard to issues such as fundraising and the pay of senior staff.[1] Another factor is the growth in the importance of diversity and equality issues, as the UK's population has become more multicultural and people require greater gender equality. A further change has been the growth of service user involvement in nonprofit organizations, including at Board level. Some, such as St Mungos, also have a policy of recruiting more former service users as staff, initially as apprentices (St Mungos 2015). In addition most nonprofits have significant service user involvement, at many different levels, including board level.

Staffing is invariably both your biggest cost and your greatest headache, unfortunately with no easy solutions. Large organizations will have HR departments that carry out most of the work required and should provide a degree of objectivity. Small organizations invariably do not have a specialist HR department, which means that managers have to carry out some or even all the HR work. However it is absolutely essential that organizations follow both good practice and the law, even though the amount of employment-related legislation and regulation has increased substantially over the last two decades.

Some desk-based research carried out a few years ago found that even small UK community organizations may be subject to over 1,500 separate pieces of legislation and regulation, around half of which was employment related (Community Matters 2009) and since then pensions have been expanded. However HR information, polices, and forms can all be easily bought online from private companies and a very useful U.S. resource is Guidestar[2] while in the UK the NCVO specializes in support for nonprofits.[3] One big advantage of these online resources is that they are invariably free, their information is written by HR professionals and they are updated regularly to take account of any new legal requirements.

There are also private online HR companies, supplying up-to-date information and polices, customized to your organization for a fee. These may be the best solution to ease the work load on managers of small organizations.

---

1 https://www.theguardian.com/voluntary-sector-network/2013/aug/06/charity-fat-cats-paid-too-much

2 http://www.guidestar.org/Home.aspx

3 https://knowhownonprofit.org/tools-resources/hr-policies

The Right Team

One of the keys to successful management in all sectors is getting the right team to work with you in the organization. Jim Collins has elaborated on this aspect in his books on companies and the Voluntary and Community Sector (Collins 2006); he writes "Those who build great organizations make sure they have the right people on the bus, the wrong people off the bus and the right people in the key seats before they figure out where to drive the bus." In other words the best managers select the right team, then involve the team in planning the project; the overall concept and direction may already have been decided but getting the team involved in the planning ensures a greater span of ideas, empowers the individual team members and gains their commitment to the project.

The Recruitment Process

Before staff are recruited, the manager must prepare a range of papers and processes. Organizations must be aware they have a legal responsibility to ensure no unlawful discrimination occurs in recruitment and selection on the grounds of sex, race, disability, age, sexual orientation and religion or belief, pregnancy, maternity, marriage and civil partnership, and gender reassignment. If the process is unfair then this can be grounds for legal action, so you must get it right; staff selection is subject to government regulation and legislation, eleven acts or regulations in the UK.

The recruitment process should cover:

- Defining the service you need, analyzing the job, the salary, and the necessary skills and experience required.
- Preparing a job description and person specification.
- Advertising vacancies.
- Interviewing, selecting and hiring staff.
- Inducting the new staff into their role and supervising their probationary periods.

A business start-up service (Shell Livewire Business Library[4]) states:

[4] https://www.shell-livewire.org/listing/business-library

Recruitment and selection can be seen as a two-stage process: Recruitment attracts the optimum number of suitably qualified candidates to apply for the post; and, selection filters this potentially large group through a variety of criteria in order to determine their suitability to match the needs of the job and the business. Recruitment and selection must be considered as two separate processes, otherwise one or both may fail. If you filter wrongly at recruitment, you may end up with a pool of poor candidates. If you attract wrongly at selection, you may end up with a poor fit between the job and the job-holder.

Job Descriptions and Person Specifications

It is essential to think through exactly what the staff role will entail; job design should produce an appropriate description of the skills and competences, knowledge and experience required for different posts. The job description outlines the tasks and responsibilities required for the role. The person specification, which should cover the tasks and responsibilities in the job description, should be an objective document, outlining the competences, knowledge, attitudes, and experience required for the role. These are normally separated out into essential and desirable attributes, which can then be used for scoring on each attribute but it can also be useful as a document to enable potential candidates to consider their own suitability and to make their application relevant to what is required.

Advertising will be important though most jobs in the economy are filled by word of mouth and internal promotion. Often there are candidates within the organization who are ready to take the next step. Networking and putting jobs onto bulletin boards and LinkedIn can spread the recruitment net wider.

Selection

Selecting and recruiting the right team needs to be rigorous and thorough, but in reality it is still a very difficult process; one experienced manager once said that the chances of selecting the right candidate at formal interviews was like sticking a pin in list of names; so probationary periods are essential (see the following). Some managers believe in offering short-term contracts to assess the standard of candidates more thoroughly. It becomes more difficult when selection boards disagree among themselves; even if they are meant to be applying objective criteria, subjectivity invariably creeps in.

The selection process should use a variety of methods, including tests, interviews, mock exercises, and meeting clients or service users. No post should be offered before taking up references and some managers always try to talk to referees over the phone to get nuances about people' performance. One useful maxim is "if in doubt do not appoint."

Recruiting Volunteers

With volunteers the process must be similar but different; job descriptions and specifications should be drawn up but clearly there is more risk of volunteers staying only a short time and the effort of recruitment being wasted. Advice and guidance is available from national nonprofit support organizations in the U.S.[5] and UK,[6] while regional and local networks often provide useful resources or help recruit and support in the UK[7] or U.S.[8] There is also a UK Quality Mark specifically for employing volunteers.[9]

Probation and Induction

In addition the process of "getting the right people on the bus" will need to include stringent use of probationary periods to test out whether staff are suitable for their roles, normally over the first 6 months. Another way is offering short-term contracts to test out suitability, or going through agencies for temporary to permanent contracts.

---

5 https://www.idealist.org

6 https://www.ncvo.org.uk/practical-support/information/volunteer-management

7 https://www.ncvo.org.uk/ncvo-volunteering/find-a-volunteer-centre

8 http://www.pointsoflight.org/handsonnetwork

9 https://iiv.investinginvolunteers.org.uk/

Induction is also important, particularly if you are recruiting young inexperienced staff. One manager always used to state it was better to recruit inexperienced people with great potential and then train them up to the right methods and standards for their organization.

Staff Handbook

At an early stage it is essential to write up a staff handbook for the organization, outlining staff hours, conditions of service, pension, collective bargaining, employment contracts, disciplinary procedures, employee involvement, equal opportunity and diversity, flexible working, grievance procedures, health and safety, holidays and time off, job sharing, pay, pensions, grading, and notice periods. There are templates which can be adapted.[10,11] This can be changed as conditions and organizations change, so it is sensible to print any hard copies as loose leaf binders so updates can be inserted.

If your organization is involved in construction or maintenance work, or risky work, you will need a comprehensive health and safety manual, with additional training for staff and trainees. Likewise this is needed if your organization provides services that place staff or service users at risk in any way such as hostels or outreach work, or where you are working with risky clients.

Staff Participation

Charles Handy (Handy 2006), a perceptive writer on organizational management, believed "It is only common sense that people are more likely to be committed to a cause if they have had a hand in shaping it" and that "Groups are likely to produce better result than the same individuals working on their own, though teams of all-stars are not always or even often the best teams. The egos get in the way of the sharing."

---

[10] https://www.nonprofithr.com/portfolio/essential-nonprofit-employee-handbook-template/

[11] https://knowhownonprofit.org/people/employment-law-and-hr/policies-and-templates/handbook

In fact engagement, empowerment, or participation must also include engagement with consumers and service users, (dealt with in Equal Opportunities chapter). The nonprofit sector has a great deal of experience in this whole area. However sometimes never-ending consultations seem to stymie any real action leading to unsatisfactory compromise, but this is often a sign of opposition to change from vested interests within an organization. This may be because the right steps have not been followed.

Staff Motivation

Motivating staff is absolutely key but there are no simple, sure fire solutions, but managers should always be working on this as it is clear that motivated staff produce better performance. Managers talk about different ways to motivate different staff; one way is getting to know individual staff and then applying "different strokes for different folks" or utilizing situational leadership (see Managing Resources chapter), allowing experienced and independent staff more scope than newer less experienced staff. Another tactic is the "feedback sandwich," that is when you need to correct or be critical of someone's behavior or performance, you also find something to praise about their work.

It is essential to set up a culture where staff are encouraged to contribute ideas, as they often have the best perspective about where the organization should be going and how best to improve results. Team meetings are a good strategy (see Managing Resources chapter).

Motivation

One big motivating factor can be the competitiveness of staff; according to Professor Ian Larkin (Larkin 2012), staff's natural tendency is to measure their own performance against the performance of others. This is both within a team and against competing organizations.

Organizations should pay the going rate to recruit good staff and then to retain them as they become more experienced. Pay rates must be fair and transparent, so the structure and rationale can be explained if challenged. But as I say in the Business Planning chapter, the staff pay structure should also be closely linked to performance, both of individual staff and of the company as a whole, rather than just recruiting staff on salaries with automatic increments.

Most staff in nonprofit organizations are altruistic, wanting to help society in some way or other. Research on public service (Ashraf, Bandiera and Jack 2014) found that

> First, non-financial rewards are more effective at eliciting effort than either financial rewards or the volunteer contract, and are also the most cost-effective...... Second, non-financial rewards leverage intrinsic motivation and, contrary to existing laboratory evidence, financial incentives do not appear to crowd it out...... Overall, the findings demonstrate the power of non-financial rewards to motivate agents in settings where there are limits to the use of financial incentives.

Staff Learning

Peter Drucker (Drucker 1990) argues that "CVOs (Community and Voluntary Organizations) need to be learning organizations… to be information based…structured around information that flows up from the individuals doing the work to the people at the top and on around information flowing down too." The flow of information is essential because a CVO has to be a learning organization. People throughout the CVO need to ask: "What do I have to learn?" "What does this CVO have to learn?"

Ian Williams (Williams 2007), in a comprehensive summary of UK nonprofit operations, writes "Without learning at different levels in a CVO there is no innovation, change and growth in impact, influence, scale, and scope of operation. Questioning and improving how a CVO learns needs to be continually advanced and specifically included in the organization's strategy."

Training should be high standard and targeted at staff facing similar issues and needing similar training: training is at its best when you are with people of similar ability; like tennis playing with more experienced people is not invigorating, nor is playing people who are much worse.

Training should not just be "sheep-dipping," processing large numbers staff quickly through courses; there is a danger that a great deal of training now seems to be about ticking boxes and ensuring compliance with tendering requirements. There is sometimes too little consideration in design and delivery of courses of how different are everyone's capabilities and requirements. This has worsened with the introduction of some poor online training; staff tell each other the shortcuts to complete these courses quickly because they are too rigid and unsophisticated, lacking application to real situations.

Staff training and continuous professional development need to be structured into annual appraisals to assess progress and suggest appropriate courses. If retraining was not considered for someone who underperforms, this can be grounds for suing for constructive dismissal.

Staff Performance

Peter Drucker (Drucker 1990) states that CVOs need to give priority to performance and results as he felt that in general they tend not to give enough emphasis to this (He was writing before output related contracts were brought in). He believed that performance and results are far more important—and far more difficult to measure and control—in CVOs than in a business. Performance is the ultimate test of an organization, as very CVO exists for the sake of performing well in changing people and society. "The ultimate question which I think everyone in the CVO should ask again and again and again, both of themselves and the organization is: "what should I hold myself accountable for by way of contribution and results?"" And then of the CVO: "What should this organization hold itself accountable for by way of contribution and results?"

The aim of managing performance is to manage in such a way that you improve the performance of both staff and that of the organization continuously. It involves making sure that the performance of employees contributes to the goals of their teams and the business as a whole.

You as the manager must generate an atmosphere of high standard performance in the team; some of this will be team work, some will be motivating individual staff, some will be developing a structure in which the manager gives regular feedback on performance in appraisals, some will be in the pay structure (see Business Plans), some will be that staff feel they themselves are contributing ideas to the organization; there is some evidence that pioneering projects produce better results, presumably because of better staff motivation.

Performance Management

To manage staff performance effectively, it is essential that managers set an example themselves. The Macleod Report[12] recommends that managers should:

- Behave in a consistent way.
- Ensure work is designed efficiently and effectively and provide clarity about what is required from people.
- Provide regular performance feedback and coaching.
- Facilitate and empower rather than control and restrict.
- Understand their people as people and know what makes them tick.
- Treat people fairly, with respect and appreciation.
- Are committed to developing and rewarding their people.
- Get the best out individuals and the team.
- Work at being inspirational role models for their people.

Strategy to Engage Staff

Although there is no master model for successful staff engagement, the Macleod Report suggested that there were four common themes from their research. The key elements to support successful employee engagement were:

- **Strategic narrative;** visible, empowering leadership providing a strong strategic narrative about the organization, where it's come from and where it's going.
- **Engaging managers** who focus their people and give them scope, treat their people as individuals and coach and stretch their people.

[12] http://engageforsuccess.org/engaging-for-success

- **Employee voice** throughout the organizations, for reinforcing and challenging views, between functions and externally. Employees are seen not as the problem, rather as central to the solution, to be involved, listened to, and invited to contribute their experience, expertise and ideas.
- **Organizational integrity**—the values on the wall are reflected in day to day behaviors. There is no "say –do" gap. Promises made and promises kept, or an explanation given as to why not.

Managing Teams Remotely

Some teams are dispersed around several locations, with some staff working from home sometimes. In these cases new media becomes useful for communication and support; a midwives social enterprise uses WhatsApp to share information and good practice. However in some cases it is essential to set up face-to-face team meetings; a recruitment company found that performance improved after this was introduced.[13]

Assessing Poor Performance and Inappropriate Behavior

Occasionally an individual staff member is not performing their job unsatisfactorily over time. Or someone may be displaying inappropriate behavior at work. Both these can have a very detrimental effect on other staff, particularly if this is not taken up by management.

First make absolutely sure there is a real issue about someone's poor performance. Record events and timescales in great detail in contemporaneous notes, otherwise you will lose out legally. Also you must follow your organization's disciplinary code and employees' contracts.

To make sure you are dealing with a real problem, make sure you can answer these questions:

1. Do you know exactly what the behavior is and how it is below standard? Can you define exactly is causing concern? Could you describe

[13] http://timewise.co.uk/knowledge/research/

it to a third party? Feelings are not enough; any specific examples with evidence rather than generalized assertions?

2. Is this behavior causing a problem? Is the behavior just irritating or is it having a definite impact on the service? Is time and money being wasted in a quantifiable way? Are other staff clearly and justifiably being upset?
3. Would other managers see this behavior in the same way? Are you interpreting this the right way? Would another manager accept your concerns as reasonable?
4. Are you being overdemanding or taking something personally? An example could be one's personal dislike of untidy desks, which doesn't always mean that the person is disorganized. You could be putting too much emphasis on too little evidence and personal idiosyncrasies.

Only when you have satisfied yourself in all four areas is it time for action. You must demonstrate this behavior is detrimental to the organization and be sure that you are dealing with a real problem which others would see objectively in the same light.

Reasons for Poor Performance

There can be a range of reasons for poor performance which you will need to properly consider. These include:

- **Personal ability:** Has the individual the right skills? Is there a skills gap needing training?
- **Manager ability:** Have you given enough direction, and made sufficient support and resources available?
- **Process gap:** Have the goalposts moved to make a task unattainable? Have there been regular enough reviews and sufficient training on offer?
- **Organizational forces:** Has the organization created red tape overkill, cultural restrictions, or hidden agendas which make the task impossible?

- **Personal circumstances:** Has something at home affected performance at work?
- **Motivation:** Is the person demotivated or suffering from stress or lack of challenge?

Managing Poor Performance

When you are satisfied you are being objective about poor performance, the steps the manager needs to take are as follows:

- Discuss the issue with the staff member concerned, providing feedback.
- Try to get to the root of the issue.
- Explore the options and alternatives available.
- Agree the next steps and clear objectives to improve, with regular meetings to check progress.
- Provide additional training and coaching if appropriate.
- Monitor and document progress.
- Help them or help them out; don't ignore the problem.

Discipline

If staff disciplinary action is required, this can be a tricky area unless you follow your organization's disciplinary code to the letter, as well as employers' contracts, and current legal requirements. Wherever possible ask for HR support at an early stage where it exists in the organization and if not there are specialist lawyers available. Union reps may need to be involved in any meetings (A performance monitoring and management system in the nonprofit sector is included as an appendix to this chapter.).

Managing Volunteers

Volunteer input and commitment is an enormous part of the nonprofit sector, arguably both its greatest strength and resource. The American Red Cross has 500,000 volunteers along with 30,000 staff, while the UK

Samaritans has over 21,000 volunteers in 200 branches. Thus, managing their recruitment, deployment, work and support is an essential but specialist skill in nonprofit sector organizations.

Any organization working with vulnerable adults or children should also have proper vetting and criminal record checking procedures in place for volunteers (and staff of course), along with a relevant program of induction and training. Another issue is retention, as the turnover for younger volunteers can be very high as they enter full-time employment, while consulting volunteers on policy matters can also become important.

Possibly the most significant group of volunteers are of course nonprofit trustees, whose recruitment and roles are vital; this subject is covered in the Governance chapter.

Some nonprofit organizations appoint specialist volunteer coordinators to recruit and support volunteers; while others develop structures with designated "lead" senior volunteers, to train new volunteers and set an example; one such organization is the British Red Cross. Certain nonprofits contract out their volunteer recruitment to specialist nonprofits, such as Volunteer Match.[14] While volunteers will not have the same employment rights or financial benefits, such as pensions, it is important to make sure that they are treated properly and with respect. Any expenses need to be sorted out in a rational and transparent system. As already stated advice is available from national nonprofit support organizations in the U.S.[15] and UK.[16]

Conclusion

Managers need to set up in their organizations the appropriate HR structures to run effectively and to develop; luckily there is great deal of free assistance for this available through networks as well as those that charge for their services. This must be a priority even in small organizations otherwise staff will not flourish or remain.

---

[14] https://www.volunteermatch.org/

[15] https://www.idealist.org

[16] https://www.ncvo.org.uk/practical-support/information/volunteer-management

References and Further Reading

ACEVO. 2006. *"Doing Good and Doing Well - Defining and Measuring Success in the Third Sector."*

Ashraf, N., O. Bandiera, and B.K. Jack. 2014. *"No Margin, No Mission? A Field Experiment on Incentives for Public Service Delivery."*

Clarke, Nita; 2013. Interview co-author "*Engage for Success*"; Great Workplace Special Report, Guardian.

Collins, J. C., and Collins, J. C. 2005. *Good to great and the social sectors: why business thinking is not the answer: a monograph to accompany.* Boulder, CO: J. Collins.

Community Matters. 2009. *A Vision for Neighbourhoods*, Report accessed in 2015; Communities Matters has now closed down.

Daily Telegraph. 2013. http://www.telegraph.co.uk/finance/newsbysector/retailandconsumer/10146737/Google-brand-damaged-by-tax-row.html

Drucker, P. 1990. *Managing the Non-Profit Organization; Practices and Principles.* New York: Harper Collins.

Furedi, F., and Bristow, J. 2012. *The Social Cost of Litigation.* London, England: London Centre for Policy Studies.

Handy, C.B. 2006. *Myself and other more important matters.* London: William Heinemann.

Landström, H. 2005. *Pioneers in Entrepreneurship and Small Business Research.* New York: Springer Science+Business Media,

Larkin J. 2012. "The Most Powerful Workplace Motivator." http://studymode.com/essays/The-Most-Powerful-Workplace-Motivator-1097447.html

St Mungos 2015 http://www.mungosbroadway.org.uk/apprenticeship_scheme

Williams, I. 2007. "The Nature of Highly Effective Community and Voluntary Organizations" http://www.dochas.ie/sites/default/files/Williams_on_Effective_CVOs.pdf

APPENDIX

Performance Monitoring System

"Doing Good and Doing Well—Defining and Measuring Success in the Third Sector" (ACEVO 2006). In this report, 10 recommendations were made for developing a sound performance monitoring and management system:

(i) Keep it Simple, performance management systems can be too complex, generating information that is neither usable nor valuable–whatever you do keep it simple.
(ii) Choose a few indicators on which progress would really make a difference.
(iii) Involve and motivate staff.
(iv) Involve service users.
(v) Negotiate with funding bodies regarding their requirements.
(vi) Integrate the performance management process into the regular planning process.
(vii) Think about appropriate systems for external verification.
(viii) Benchmark—a valuable way to promote peer learning and identifying issues that need attention.
(ix) Find the resources to do the job.
(x) Finally, know what's going on—vision must be accompanied by practical understanding. Don't chase abstract goals or have your heads in the clouds as you must know what is going on at the frontline.

CHAPTER 10

Equal Opportunity, Diversity, and Service User Involvement

Don Macdonald and Sue Causton

Overview

This chapter analyzes different facets of equality and diversity, including the legal basis and the business case to implement these. It examines ways of devising and implementing suitable and relevant policies, while describing different methods to involve service users; all of these have become essential in today's nonprofit organization.

Introduction

Equality and diversity are absolutely crucial precepts to be fully understood and followed in pursuing management in the nonprofit sector, where organizations are promoting the cause of disadvantaged groups and at the same time fighting inequality and discrimination. Involving service users in the organization in different ways is a separate but related part of the equation of setting up and sustaining a fair, responsive, and effective nonprofit organization.

Without effective practice in these areas, organizations will not be considered legitimate, neither will they generate the greatest commitment and most effective effort from staff, volunteers, and stakeholders, nor will they gain proper feedback to inform good practice and policy. Besides as described in the following, discrimination is illegal.

So all these factors should be properly considered and thought through in depth at an organizational level, but individual managers also need to carefully consider their own views and eliminate any prejudices. For the organization, policies need to be drawn up and then integrated into the core functions of the organization, in terms of responding to the needs of staff, stakeholders (including volunteers), and service users. Such policies are also required by most funders and commissioners, while a strong business case in their favor also exists (see the following).

Definitions

The concept of equality provides a framework to protect against discrimination, promote equality of opportunity, and foster good relations between people with different characteristics. Diversity is the valuing of our individual differences and talents, creating a culture where everyone can participate, thrive, and contribute.

Legislation and Other Measures

Legislation has been implemented in almost all Western countries to outlaw discrimination, since the U.S. Supreme Court's 1954 Brown vs. Board of Education decision furthered government initiatives to end discrimination, and also the landmark U.S. Civil Rights Act in 1964. However it has been backed by other government action, such as the U.S. Federal Government's threat to cut off funding that forced the desegregation of schools in the South, while Supreme Court decisions on affirmative action programs have ensured that minorities have been assisted to progress in a whole range of areas. (Reynolds 2010).

The changes in the U.S. came about because of long and painful campaigns mounted by leaders such as Martin Luther King, individuals, such as Rosa Parks, and associations, such as the Freedom Riders and NACCAP,[1] along with political maneuvers by President Johnson (Caro 2014). "The rights revolution of the 1960s changed the landscape and language of American politics" and also "caught the imagination of the world and encouraged emulation by other 'rights' movements including those of women" (Reynolds 2010).

One could argue that matters have progressed so much that public opinion and pressure from the corporate sector achieve most: the ejection of the powerful newsreader, Bill O'Reilly from Fox News in 2017, because of sexual harassment allegations, demonstrated the influence from the public along with companies who were not prepared to advertise with the network.

Current legislation in the U.S. is enforced by the Equal Employment Opportunities Commission (EEOC).[2] Most employers with at least 15 employees are covered by EEOC laws... which apply to all types of work situations, including hiring, firing, promotions, harassment and training. Under federal laws, employees include:

- People who work full-time, part-time, seasonally, or on a temporary basis
- Volunteers
- Workers assigned through a work program
- Workers who aren't U.S. citizens, including those who are undocumented

[1] http://www.naacp.org/

[2] https://www.eeoc.gov/

U.S. state governments also have extensive laws so check your state and local government websites for specific information; for example, some states prohibit discrimination on the basis of:

- Marital status
- Sexual orientation
- Gender identity or cross-dressing
- Legal off-duty conduct, such as smoking
- Whistleblowing
- Taking leave to vote, serve on a jury or be a witness in a legal proceeding

In the UK laws are enforced by the Equal Opportunities Commission (EOC) and these apply across the UK, with some exceptions in Northern Ireland.[3] UK legislation protects individuals from unfair treatment, advances equality of opportunity for all and promotes a fair and more equal society. The aim is to ensure that public bodies play their part in making society fairer and this includes nonprofit organizations performing public functions or services. This could include—for example:

- Organizations who have been subcontracted to carry out a public function like job seeking services
- Housing associations when carrying out some of their functions as a social landlord
- Nonprofit sector organizations providing care or other services on behalf of the local authorities or the NHS
- Private organizations and charities which carry out public functions are called hybrid authorities.

The Duty now covers the following "protected characteristics":

- Age
- Disability
- Gender reassignment
- Pregnancy and maternity

---

[3] http://www.eoc.org.uk

- Race (including ethnic or national origins, color or nationality
- Religion or belief (including lack of belief)
- Sex
- Sexual orientation
- Marriage and civil partnership

Public bodies are required to have *due regard* for the need to: eliminate unlawful discrimination, advance equality of opportunity, and foster good relations.

Monitoring Requirements

Most funders, both public and trusts, have requirements for measuring equality and diversity in projects they fund, including recruitment and outcomes. Organizations in receipt of funds have to ensure they have set up systems to monitor these in order to provide this information (for example ethnic or gender breakdown of service users) and when they report on their project outputs. Most funders require organizations to have equal opportunity and diversity policies in place.

Business Case for Diversity

There is also a "business case" for diversity. A UK report by the Chartered Institute of Personnel and Development sets out the key business benefits for developing diversity orientated organizations. These include:

- Greater access to different perspectives and sources of information
- Greater understanding of customers
- Better communication with customers
- Increased legitimacy

The findings from Thomson Reuters' reports[4] clearly connect authentically diverse workplaces with positive financial performance, including:

---

[4] https://blogs.thomsonreuters.com/answerson/business-case-for-diversity

- Workplace diversity is the foundation to power innovation.
- Workplace diversity for diversity's sake won't fly.
- The importance of authenticity (beyond hitting a number).
- Diversity and inclusion: you can't have one without the other.

And finally work undertaken by the Confederation for British Industry set out three key business drivers namely:

- Increasing employee satisfaction, which helps attract new staff and retain those already there, reduces recruitment costs, and can increase productivity
- Understanding better how the company's diverse customers think and what drives their spending habits, or how to access markets they have not previously been able to tap into so effectively
- Finding enough workers to fill skills gaps in areas with tight labor markets, where there are not enough "obvious candidates" for the vacancies they have

Understanding Diversity

The concept of diversity encompasses acceptance and respect. It means understanding that each individual is unique, and recognizing our individual differences. These can be along the dimensions of race, ethnicity, gender, sexual orientation, socioeconomic status, age, physical abilities, religious beliefs, political beliefs, or other ideologies. It is the exploration of these differences in a safe, positive, and nurturing environment. It is about understanding each other and moving beyond simple tolerance to embrace and celebrate the rich dimensions of diversity of each individual.

Diversity is a reality created by individuals and groups from a broad spectrum of demographic and philosophical differences. It is extremely important to support and protect diversity by valuing individuals and groups free from prejudice, and by fostering a climate where equity and mutual respect are intrinsic.

Diversity means more than just acknowledging or tolerating differences. It is a set of conscious practices that involve:

- Understanding and appreciating interdependence of humanity, cultures, and the natural environment
- Practicing mutual respect for qualities and experiences that are different from our own
- Understanding that diversity includes not only ways of being but also ways of knowing
- Recognizing that personal, cultural, and institutionalized discrimination creates and sustains privileges for some, while creating and sustaining disadvantages for others
- Building alliances across differences so that we can work together to eradicate all forms of discrimination

The Diversity Assessment Tests

Therefore diversity includes knowing how to relate to those qualities and conditions that are different from our own and outside the groups to which we belong, yet are present in other individuals and groups. These include but are not limited to all the different aforelisted qualities.

Some organizations that aspire to move toward embracing diversity and equality fully choose to use diversity assessment tests to enable them to:

- Benchmark themselves against a clear model of best practice of diversity as it relates to business operations.
- Develop standards for the measurement and reporting of diversity initiatives.
- Engage in a common framework for discussion between different parts of the same organization, including those operations in different countries.
- Create a clear "leadership framework" for diversity which can operate across the organization.
- Identify key areas for the development of strategies and initiatives for best practice.

The assessment tests are essentially a survey of perceptions that can be conducted internally as part of regular internal climate surveys and externally as a way to gauge external stakeholder perceptions and reputation with the general public. It measures:

- Five levels of the Equity Continuum as described earlier
- Organizational processes
- Organizational activities
- Matrix—activity and validation statements

Managing Diversity

Trying to manage diversity by improving representation should also include culture change, involving everyone and the whole social system of organizations.

In all kinds of organizations, managing diversity effectively involves bringing on and encouraging the talent from both mainstream and minority groups into maximum development and contribution at all levels. It should recognize originality while respecting origins. It is also about bridging and building relationships through sensible mechanisms that challenge barriers and provide opportunities for individual and organizational effectiveness.

How it works is that if an organization wants to improve its diversity and equality, it should:

1. Commit itself to improve its performance in that area
2. Work up an Equal Opportunity and Diversity Policy outlining the overall objectives and tasks
3. Develop a *strategy and plan* outlining the specific steps to implement this
4. Design some outcomes to measure effectiveness
5. Deliver its plan
6. Evaluate the results and achievements
7. Review and realign the processes
8. Repeat regularly as necessary

Equal Opportunity Policy

Examples of comprehensive equal opportunity and diversity policies can be easily found to be used as a model to develop your own;[5] likewise

[5] http://southwestforum.org.uk/sites/default/files/sitefiles/docs/eq_policy.pdf

advice and guidance is available to cover the right areas and to take you through the right procedures. Care should be taken to find ones that are applicable to the size and focus of your organization. Many large organizations have specialist equality and diversity teams, so their capacity is way beyond that of a small organization. Informality is an important ingredient in how small organizations manage themselves, but it is still essential for credibility let alone equality and diversity for small organizations to take this issue very seriously.

Service User Involvement

There are many good reasons to involve service users and careers in a variety of ways in nonprofit organizations. These include:

- To give people a real say in the services on offer and the way they are provided
- To better adapt your services to meet peoples' individual needs
- To make sure your organization provides good quality services that are friendly, fair, and useful
- To make sure your services support people's dignity and independence
- To make sure that the services you provide continue to give people the things that they want
- To make sure your organization continues to improve in all areas

Service User Involvement in Health and Social Care

Over the last decades there has been a strong push for service user involvement in health and social care from many different directions, including from service users themselves. Large UK charities, such as Leonard Cheshire Disability have been criticized for not doing enough in the past, although their new chief executive, who is himself disabled, has pledged to do much more.[6]

---

[6] https://theguardian.com/society/2016/oct/11/neil-heslop-disability-rights-benefit-assessment-government-leonard-cheshire

However there can be difficulties guaranteeing that any involvement is real and not just tokenistic. Another danger is if the new structures just involve the articulate service users who invariably make their voices heard anyway.

A UK report, *Beyond the Usual Suspects: Towards Inclusive Involvement*, edited by Peter Beresford,[7] himself a former service user, found that involvement of service users was positive, with close relationship between finding the time and money to enable organizations to listen and making any listening exercise work effectively.

Involvement Process

So it is important for organizations to clarify the roles that service users can usefully and realistically perform. This planning needs to take account of the size, scope, and function of the organization, and how this is reflected in its service users.

The ways that service users can be involved include:

- Acting as a trustee or committee member
- Volunteering, particularly in peer-to-peer projects
- Advising and giving feedback on new and existing projects
- Working on social media for the organization
- Helping with fundraising

Youth councils are an example of how this can be structured and also how useful this can be; Chicago YMCA run youth leadership programs.[8]

Another important development is the deployment of expert patients' programs by organizations such as PatientsLikeMe a U.S.-based online community[9] which enables patients to meet others with similar conditions and share their experience. One review found that patients better adhered to medication and needed fewer visits to hospitals as a result.

---

7 http://shapingourlives.org.uk/documents/BTUSReport.pdf

8 http://ymcachicago.org/southside/programs/youth-and-teen-leadership/

9 https://patientslikeme.com/

Barriers

If service users involved in structures believe that no one is actually listening to them or acting on what they say, then they often drop out of any consultation process. As Beresford says "The people who are most likely to do this are the most excluded, the most disempowered: those whose voices particularly need to be heard."

Beresford describes how people with complex and multiple impairments are often left out, because their involvement is seen as too expensive or difficult. The same happens where people are seen as awkward or difficult; for example, the growing number of people with dementia and people who include themselves within the range of neuro-diversity. Service users frequently comment that some points of view are more welcome than others—particularly those of people who agree with what's on offer. According to Beresford "More confident and assertive service users are often unpopular among those organizing involvement activities, and can be dismissed as the usual suspects."

Overcoming Barriers

Overcoming these barriers is essential. One of the strengths of most non-profit organizations is that close involvement with service users exists already and this can be expanded for this purpose.

Some service users will need training and support to become fully involved. Some people do not have an understanding of meeting behavior and protocols, while for others speaking in large or formal meetings is problematic. If training does not always succeed, setting up other communication channels should be considered, including smaller more informal group discussions, customer panels, mystery shopping, feedback surveys, and online discussion groups; these can be one way to bypass these blockages.

The Beyond The Usual Suspects project offers evidence and practical help which is freely available to help everyone working for effective and inclusive user involvement. There are also other helpful agencies to build on to enable diverse involvement such as National Survivor User Network's National Involvement Standards and the Care Quality Commission).

Of course many nonprofit organizations are service user led. However for small organizations particularly, introducing service user involvement for the first time should be carefully thought through as it does require additional resources and needs measures, such as training and new policies, around confidentiality.

Concluding Comments

Equality has improved immensely in the U.S. since the 1960s, with improvements in income and education. However Black unemployment remains twice the level of White unemployment, similar to where it was in 1972, while African Americans have not caught up to White and Asian people in educational attainment.[10] The Black Lives Matter campaign shows the ongoing concern about police brutality. The UK is still very divided by class as a recent report on social mobility led by a former cabinet minister suggests; many groups do less well in the UK education system; for example, working-class boys, while young black men are over-represented in the prison system. Although part of the UK, Northern Ireland, does not allow same sex marriages and abortions are restricted. In parts of the world homosexuality is still punished by death.

The glass ceiling still restricts opportunities for women and black people in Western society. We assume this situation also prevails to a large degree in the nonprofit sector, reflecting power in society and the political elite. Even though advocates of social enterprise state that more women are CEOs in this sector, other research shows they still earn less than their male equivalents. Yet much can still be achieved.

The progress engineered by the strong Lesbian Bisexual Gay and Transgender (LBGT) movements in the U.S. and the UK over the last 20 years on a wide range of issues (including rights, marriage, adoption, pardons) shows what can be achieved through sophisticated organizing and effective campaigning. However this has clearly been successful because of the resources generated and the sophistication of the lobbying.

---

[10] https://usatoday.com/story/news/nation/2014/01/19/civil-rights-act-progress/4641967/

One advantage of being a small organization is that you can be more imaginative and move in more radical directions, unencumbered by cumbersome structures in order to overcome inequality and promote diversity. As Shift MS, a small UK charity, states "One of the benefits of being small is that you're more able to speak directly with your community." Social media can also enable you to set up two ways communication, more promptly and flexibly with service users.

Managers must take responsibility and set a lead within their organizations, making clear what they expect in all spheres. This will be helped by developing a strategy and plan (as outlined earlier), to encompass the whole organization. There is a need to ensure that trustees and staff reflect the diversity of the communities the organization is working with, that there is engagement with a wide range of stakeholders and mechanisms in place to ensure engagement with service users.

If your organization delivers services on behalf of a "public body," for example, home care services for UK local government, you will be deemed a "hybrid authority" and expected from the outset to monitor equality targets and outputs set as part of your contract. It is imperative therefore that you have monitoring structures in place before you bid for contracts.

Managers will need to work hard to get all this organized and working smoothly, so ongoing training and support is a vital component. It is worthwhile being affiliated to a national support body such as the NCVO (UK)[11] or the National Council of Non Profits (U.S.).[12] They provide training courses, consultancy and up-to-date news. An alternative is to join generalist networks such as the Inclusiveness Project (U.S.)[13] or more specialist networks such as the Equality Network, a U.S. grassroots organization for the lesbian, gay, bisexual, transgender and queer community[14] or sector-based networks in UK Further Education.[15]

The nonprofit sector has for decades led the way in combating inequality and poverty, by understanding and taking on board the needs

---

[11] https://www.ncvo.org.uk/

[12] https://www.councilofnonprofits.org

[13] http://www.nonprofitinclusiveness.org/

[14] http://www.equalitynetwork.org

[15] http://www.equalitynetwork.co.uk/

of the communities we work in and developing innovative projects and services that meet those needs. In the current economic and political climate, now more than ever, we need to ensure we continue to work with diverse communities, providing real opportunities and choices. There is still a great deal to be done as stated earlier, but equality and diversity are the most important principles that should underpin our nonprofit organization's work.

References and Further Reading

Caro, R. 2014. *The Years of Lyndon Johnson; Volume 4.* New York: Random House.

Reynolds, D. 2010. *America, Empire of Liberty.* London, England: Penguin Books.

This book is very useful; it is short, sharp and informative; Spencer, L. *Diversity Pocketbook.* https://www.pocketbook.co.uk/product/diversity-pocketbook/

CHAPTER 11

Communications and Marketing for Small Nonprofits

Don Macdonald

Summary

This chapter describes key aspects of communications and marketing and how to plan and implement them in a nonprofit, along with possible benefits.

Introduction

Communications and marketing are complex areas. There are marketing degree courses, while if you Google "communications for small nonprofits" you see 1.1 million links. This means there is an enormous amount of help available, but sorting out what can be useful is time-consuming, particularly if you have a press release to prepare. Digital communication opens up new channels and audiences, but an experienced communications manager says that digital is both a curse and blessing for small nonprofits; they have very tight budgets, smaller teams, and struggle to keep up with larger nonprofits.[1]

Most nonprofit organizations are small, with no specialist marketing or communications staff. So either this work is carried out by generalist staff or provided by the private sector, which could even be on a pro bono basis. Organizing your marketing and communications properly for your nonprofit brings benefits, but must be carefully planned and evaluated.

What Are Communications and Marketing?

Communications involves identifying key audiences and communicating important messages to them. Peter Drucker wrote "The aim of marketing is to know and understand the customer so well the product or service fits him and sells itself." (Drucker 1990). Ian Bruce stated "A practical definition of marketing which suits non-profits is: 'meeting customer needs within the objectives of the organization'" (Bruce 2005).

Why Do Nonprofit Organizations Need Communications and Marketing?

For many nonprofits, marketing and communications is a low priority. But effectively communicating about your organization will advance your mission.[2] In fact many nonprofit managers automatically follow good practice in this area, for instance by projecting a positive profile of their

---

[1] E-mail to author

[2] http://nonprofitanswerguide.org/marketing-communications/

organizations' work, networking, being entrepreneurial and pursuing opportunities; Shaw (2004) suggests that for "social enterprises marketing was second nature even though they did not speak of marketing or use the language of marketing."

Marketing and communications are increasing in importance for these reasons:

- Bidding for funds and contracts in the last decade becoming more competitive in the sector, with both nonprofit and private competitors raising the bar on tendering.
- Nonprofits' reputation has declined, around issues such as fundraising and high salaries.
- New media has expanded, with faster response times; young people are media savvy, utilizing new media more.

Clearly any marketing and communications plan must be appropriate to the size and mission of the nonprofit; a small local playgroup, with good community links needs a completely different approach to that of a regional organization working with young people at risk. In turn this is very different from the enormous reach of nationally recognized nonprofits, like Barnados (UK) or United Way (U.S.), while others like UNICEF have international recognition; any campaigning and education work of such organizations interact with their marketing and communications.

A Communications and Marketing Plan

Every plan should start from an analysis of the key factors affecting your nonprofit. Your organization's objectives are critical in delineating the plan: if you manage a campaigning nonprofit, clearly you put great effort into developing and delivering a communications plan that encompasses lobbying, while, if you manage a social enterprise selling goods or services to the public, you place more emphasis on market research, marketing, and sales.

A SWOT Analysis is useful, specifically around marketing and communications to identify strengths, weaknesses, opportunities, and threats, which should include your competitors, political, economic, social, and technological context, including social media. In terms of competitors you should analyze their media profile, size, scope and if possible their pricing. Remember that some commissioners prefer small local organizations to large ones muscling in. It is essential to take an honest and balanced view of where your organization stands in relation to the key opportunities and threats.

Marketing Plan

A marketing plan should analyze the operating environment, strengths and weaknesses, key audiences and outline marketing methods, covering the following points:

- What services you provide?
- Which localities you serve?
- Who are the beneficiaries and who are your customers, namely who is paying for the services?
- What are customers' main needs and wishes?
- Who is the competition and how is your service different and better?
- What prices are you charging, and compared with the competition?
- What social impact are you making and can this support your communications?
- Where should you promote your service?
- Who will provide your marketing? Do you have the expertise within the organization to market and promote your service? Or do you need assistance? (Adapted from Bruce (2005))

These questions may seem like common sense but it is essential for nonprofits to devise a marketing plan carefully.

Market Research

Markets change and evolve over time; examples are the way that sales of the Big Issue (the London newspaper sold by homeless people) have declined and now they are looking at online distribution and creating coffee and retail outlets, while Bike Works, a UK social enterprise, benefited from the increase in cycling popularity in the 21st century in London. So, good market research is critical.

Five Marketing Tips for Nonprofits

Adapted from article by Sean Horrigan

1. Produce a Brand Positioning Statement
   A nonprofit's brand is its most important asset. As well as a mission or vision statement you should have a positioning statement or strap line; a one- or two-sentence statement that articulates your organization's value, conveying succinctly who you are, what you do, and why anyone should care.
2. Invest in Good Design
   First impressions are everything. And good design ensures that your organization will always make strong first impressions in the minds of donors, prospects and volunteers.
3. Harness the Power of PR
   Powerful PR is vital component to any successful fundraising campaign. It generates brand awareness, builds buzz, and increases credibility and if your story resonates, people are going to get involved.
4. Tap into the Power of Video
   Did you know that video has a 400 percent higher engagement rate than static content? And the average website visitor spends 88 percent more time on sites that feature video?

Full article *http://nonprofithub.org/nonprofit-marketing-plan/five-marketing-mistakes-nonprofits-need-avoid*

Elinor Shaw suggests that with fewer economic assets, smaller entrepreneurial organizations use networks in which they operate to carry out relevant market research (Shaw 2004). Sometimes more formal research is required. This should cover:

- Size and scope of the market.
- Opportunities for new services.

- Customer Analysis, including preferences for services and realistic pricing, bearing in mind that the customer may be a council buying in services for clients.
- Competition evaluation.

Qualitative research is more affordable than quantitative research. Even a small phone survey of existing and potential customers provides useful feedback to underpin decisions about existing services and possible new markets.

Structuring Market Research

Ian Bruce (Bruce 2005) outlined how to structure your market research for different groups:

Existing customers

- Who are you?
- What products (or services) have you taken up?
- How much, with what usage pattern?
- What is being paid and who is paying?
- Where and how did you take up this product or service?
- When did you start?

Potential customers

- Who are you? (Sector, company position)
- Which of our products or services do you know about?
- Which might you consider taking up and why?
- Which do you definitely not want and why?
- Which of those services about which you did not know, are the most attractive and why?

Communications and Public Relations

Communications covers a wide range of aspects. Managers need to be aware how critical communications can be and that this needs careful planning and management. This may sound daunting for a small nonprofit organization but many managers are natural communicators, particularly when they are committed to and knowledgeable about a specific cause, which adds strength to any communication.

Communications and public relations (PR) are significant subjects of their own, with their own institutes and degree courses, so these paragraphs only introduce the subject. PR is essential but will be very different if your nonprofit is trying to sell services to the public, or your organization is trying to influence public opinion, social policy, or government; I am not covering the latter aspect here in great detail as I assume if this is crucial, staff with expertise will be appointed. However, in both the U.S. and UK, if your nonprofit engages in political lobbying above certain expenditure levels, you must register with the appropriate government agency.

Communications Plan

You should devise a communications plan, designed to help you and your organization communicate effectively.[3] In this you should set some specific and attainable targets to aim at (see SMART objectives in Project Management chapter), such as numbers of publicity mentions or increases in newsletter circulation, with timescales for achieving these.

Your plan should include an analysis of your stakeholders, clarifying why they might be interested in your organization (potential funders, beneficiaries), what positions they hold (government?), why your organization might be valuable to them, and any partnerships.

Key Messages and Target Groups

Key messages should be agreed, along with which target group(s) you want to reach and which media. These are related, so if you want to reach more young people you would probably use social media, whereas if you are trying to reach youth service policy makers, you would use professional press and different messages.

---

[3] http://knowhownonprofit.org/campaigns/communications/effective-communications-1/communications-plan

Deciding on and describing specific target groups is what the professionals describe as segmenting, which means you are able to move into more detailed planning.

Also you can focus your plan more by being as specific as possible. If directors in housing associations are an important target for your key messages, make a list of them and describe the channels you hope to use. In the digital age you have to fight hard for people's attention so your content should be as powerful and punchy as you can make it.

Getting a Press Release Published

Many local papers are looking for news stories, particularly good news stories, as it saves their time and effort. However, it must be sent to them in the form of a well-written press release (preferably with a picture) briefly describing an activity or achievement of your organization (see model press release in the appendix). As well as the story and picture, you must provide background information about the organization, its work, and a contact phone number. However do bear in mind that the readership will of course be predominately local.

If you are trying to target opinion formers and professionals, a good approach is to conduct research or evaluation into your organization's work, publish this in basic form, publicize this in an accompanying press release and through social media.

Public Relations for Small Nonprofits on a Shoestring Budget

Adapted from article by David Hamilton

Small charities with a smaller hierarchy than bigger charities can respond quicker, piggybacking on breaking news and more flexibly (see case study in Fundraising chapter).

Plan: Map out your key issues and choose a few topics to campaign on.

Offer life stories of your beneficiaries, giving a human angle.

To use social media platforms properly, you must invest time and effort to engage people—not just broadcast at them.

Never be afraid to get someone else to do the job for you. Half of public relations is about getting other people to repeat your messages.

Letters pages are among the most read in many publications; you must react quickly and succinctly commenting on the issue not just selling your organization.

The media prefer visual packages and photos along with any quotes or press releases.

Full article *https://theguardian.com/voluntary-sector-network/2014/apr/02/public-relations-for-small-charities-guide*

Social Media

Working with young people opens up enormous possibilities as they are so conversant with online communication and can be involved in designing and delivering peer-to-peer communication, as well as other new media.

Social media provides enormous potential, though different media should be used for different objectives and reach different audiences. A youth charity organizes its younger volunteers to develop material for social media, such as videos,[4] while others utilize social media for crowdfunding.

Networking

Networking is a natural skill for gregarious extroverts, but introverts also network when you have an exciting project or worthy cause to pursue. Building networks is a key skill in marketing, for managers which we also cover in "Managing Yourself" and the "Fundraising" chapters.

Networking includes becoming (and staying) informed about policies and key organizations and staff, identifying and communicating with stakeholders and other key individuals such as funders, making general contacts, attending conferences, while informing contacts and a wider audience about your service or project.

---

[4] https://facebook.com/LondonFootballJourneys

Eleanor Shaw (Shaw 2004) pointed out that networking was essential to nonprofits in providing "founders with information and knowledge required to identify opportunities locally," while "networks and networking were important for many of the same reasons...(namely)...acquiring market and customer information; identifying opportunities and providing introductions to possible funding sources and so on."

Conclusion

Nonprofits should utilize their social impact to communicate their achievements and activities in a positive way through a range of media. They can also use this to market their services, but this must be matched by quality and price, although there may be scope for a small mark-up on price over commercial competitors.

Resources for Communications and Marketing

Get specialist help and support by joining networks of like-minded professionals, https://ncmnetwork.org (U.S.) or http://charitycomms.org.UK **(UK) also from industry organizations like Social Media for Nonprofits** http://socialmedia4nonprofits.org **or Media Trust (UK)** http://mediatrust.org.

Tips about marketing and communications are available from CNM (U.S.) http://nonprofitanswerguide.org/marketing-communications or from NCVO (UK)

http://knowhownonprofit.org/campaigns.

References and Further Reading

Bruce, I. 2005. *Charity Marketing: Meeting Need Through Customer Focus.* London: ICSA Publishing.

Drucker, P. 1990. *Managing the Non-Profit Organization Practices and Principles.* New York: Harper Collins.

Shaw, E. 2004. "Marketing in the Social Enterprise Context: Is It Entrepreneurial?" *Qualitative Market Research: An International Journal* 7, no. 3, pp. 194–205.

APPENDIX

Specimen Local Press Release

Local Charity Pioneers Effective Methods to Combat Dementia

With an aging population, dementia is now our greatest medical challenge in the United Kingdom, but recent research shows that music and dance can be positive tools to combat its effects. These activities promote well-being and confidence, boost skills and knowledge, while giving pleasure to both participants and audiences. A project for North West London elders and those with dementia providing music and dance is being launched by the Ashford Place charity as part of a holistic approach. The charity needs to fundraise for the project, which is being supported by the best-selling author, Elizabeth Buchan https://givey.com/crickmusicanddance.

Note to Editors

With an aging population, **dementia** is now the leading cause of death in the United Kingdom according to the ONS.[5] It is therefore our greatest medical challenge, but 13 times more is spent on researching cures for cancer than on dementia even though it is more costly to the nation according to a study by Oxford University.[6] However **other research** shows that music actively promotes brain activity in dementia sufferers

[5] http://www.bbc.co.uk/news/health-37972141

[6] http://ox.ac.uk/news/2015-04-14-uk-dementia-and-stroke-research-remains-underfunded

(Alzheimer's Society[7]) while dance is the best exercise for both brain and body to prevent dementia (Massachusetts Medical Society[8]).

Ashford Place, set up in 1983, is a community charity in Cricklewood, providing a range of services for local people. http://ashfordplace.org.UK

For further information or photos please contact. **Don Macdonald** 0201 691 1234; Donmac@hotmail.com

The story was published with a photo after clarification by a journalist www.kilburntimes.co.uk/news/cricklewood-choir-to-launch-a-new-dance-project-1-4791569

---

7 http://ageuk.org.uk/health-wellbeing/conditions-illnesses/dementia-and-music/

8 http://nejm.org/doi/full/10.1056/NEJMoa022252

Final Thoughts

Don Macdonald

Unpredictable Times

We live in uncertain and unpredictable times. As Chris Birch states "Future historians will probably judge we are living through a revolution. Propelled by global forces and the push/pull of information and communications technology, our established political, economic and social models are struggling to cope." Social and technological change seems to be speeding up, while "the impact of the speed of change is perhaps what differentiates current challenges to those of the past."

The future is hard to predict; very few economists predicted the 2008 crash while many other experts consistently resisted acknowledging the rise of IT and the Internet: one scientist told the author in the mid-1980s that computers were just glorified typewriters. The then UK prime minister clearly did not foretell the Brexit vote to leave the European Union when he decided to set up a referendum in 2014, nor was the election of Donald Trump as the U.S. president in 2016 predicted by most experts or pollsters.

Opportunities

Yet these changes can also bring opportunities. For nonprofit sector organizations with the right skills and aptitude, technology opens up new services, create new fundraising channels and cut costs. For service users and staff it can open up new communication channels between each other and with the powers that be, whoever they are. Then there is Artificial Intelligence (AI), whose effect will immense. Clearly young people are better equipped to use IT and AI applications, but managers of any age can keep up by training, networking and so on.

Scrutiny

The business world is clearly much more fast-moving than the nonprofit sector. One reason is because the nonprofit sector is regulated and guided by service users' needs on the one hand, by government direction, funding, and regulations on the other hand and finally by volunteers' involvement. In other words the sector has many more stakeholders than the private sector, as discussed earlier, which leads to greater scrutiny. In turn this provokes attention from the press over issues such as fundraising methods, senior managers' pay, or the performance of individual charities.

Trends in the Sector

Political scientist and writer, Michael Kaufman, writes[1] that "Various factors have shaped the modern nonprofit sector in the U.S.:

> First and foremost, the country has a small social security net, state-funded healthcare, and state support for cultural institutions compared to other OECD countries. People's lives and well-being and the vibrancy of communities have depended on robust non-profits.
>
> Second is the massive role of organized religion which occupies a space now unknown in many European countries or Canada. Churches, mosques, synagogues, and temples, and the religious-based non-profits they support, play a critical role in social services and healthcare especially in smaller communities, although in big cities the most important non-profits and community groups are secular (I should add that this church role isn't always positive, as seen by the well-funded and well-organized groups opposing women's right to reproductive services or LGBT rights.).
>
> Third, in the absence of an adequate state role, individual charitable contributions to non-profits play a much bigger role than in most countries, as do private family foundations (from the Carnegies, Fords, Rockefellers, and Gates on down). The reasons for this are complex. When it comes to giving, U.S. residents are a very generous

[1] Private e-mail to author 2017.

> lot. Tax laws encourage donations. And there is a belief in individual action over state measures and a stress on 'charity,' as opposed to universal rights to services. But there is also a long-standing role of community-based organizations, which create person-to-person connections to meet needs outside of the state. Community foundations, for example, provide a critical response to local needs. At times their programs draw on support from city governments, which shows how complicated the picture actually is."

In the UK Peter Beresford believes that there is a growing divide between small charitable organizations—with low profile but high energy, real street credibility, and beneficiary involvement—and the traditional UK large nonprofit organizations—with big reserves, highly paid chief executives, and expensive central London headquarters.[2]

It is unclear exactly what the future will holds for the nonprofit sector in the UK. The British Council predicted in 2014 that all UK charities would generate income from contracts and trading; that is clearly unlikely for small charities but not for large ones. Grants from statutory funders will not return for the sector in place of contracts, as the latter gives much greater control to funders over service delivery. This trend also ensures that competitive tendering will continue, with requirements that impact be measured and reported in some detail. Research from NPC[3] shows that UK nonprofits are cross-subsiding state contracts with charitable donations but not always succeeding in covering their own costs; a recent example is Lifeline, a UK charity with a £62 million annual turnover, which has collapsed.[4]

Likewise the involvement of the private sector in delivering large contracts in both the U.S. and UK (for example, prisons, health care) is almost certain to continue, so many nonprofit sector organizations will inevitably carry on with subcontracting as a way of generating income for

---

[2] https://theguardian.com/society/2012/apr/24/tax-relief-row-big-charities-priorities

[3] http://thinknpc.org/

[4] https://theguardian.com/society/2017/may/18/drug-and-alcohol-charity-lifeline-project-collapses

themselves and still being able to offer services. Yet most charities are still very small with no contract income, with some subsisting solely on local fundraising or trust fund income.

Realistic Perspective

It is essential for nonprofit sector managers to develop a realistic future perspective both on a macro level—looking out for changes in the political and business environments within society—but also on a micro level—in their own organizations, to ensure they can meet new challenges. NCVO have predicted that there will be many changes in Western society and nonprofit management, including those involving new technology, social attitudes, and population demography.[5] In a useful paper, Williams notes that organizations can become more successful by spending their time improving their understanding of the likely future regarding these external pressures and using this to make a stronger organizational strategy.[6] As I have written elsewhere with a colleague "The environment is dynamic and the only thing, of which we can be sure, is that change will be continuous and demanding" and nonprofit sector managers "must be prepared for this, be always learning and be resilient."

Trends

Leading and managing a nonprofit organization is both demanding and rewarding. Managers must expect the unexpected and equip themselves to deal with whatever comes. Rising to meet such challenges is one of the aspects of management that is exciting. Clearly it is particularly stressful if it is your first management role and you are operating in the prevailing climate of austerity and cuts.

I cannot emphasize enough how essential it is to seek high quality training, support, and coaching for yourself to equip yourself to overcome

---

5 http://www.ncvo.org.uk/images/documents/policy_and_research/funding/financial-trends-for-small-and-medium-sized-charities-ncvo-lloyds-bank-foundation-2016.pdf

6 http://www.dochas.ie/sites/default/files/Williams_on_Effective_CVOs.pdf

these challenges. I have already stated how important it is to define your training needs, through some sort of training needs analysis to select what you need (see chapter Managing Your Resources). These activities overlap, in that the best training provides support, while the best coaching gives one-to-one training. Informal networking with peers in the field can also provide support and generate new ideas.

Leadership Styles

One guiding principle is to assess the situation you are facing very thoroughly, including the resources and staff you have available, the realistic prospects for your organization and then to plan and deliver from there. Clearly some leadership styles (for example, Commanding) are only best suited today to situations, where clear danger is threatened to service users, staff or public or the organization itself (which might include financial danger). Hard work always pays off; the old saying is very true, namely that genius is 99 percent perspiration, or as one head teacher states real "delivery is about grind not just the grand."

Some recent research into school leadership in the United Kingdom. The Centre for High Performance identified five types of so-called superheads of schools: "architects, soldiers, surgeons, accountants and philosophers."[7] Most of the styles were not effective over the long term, apart from the "architects," who do not opt for a short-term solution, but build schools that continue to improve long after they have left. "Rather than making quick fixes they build relationships with the local community, create a climate of respect and trust, develop their (staff's) teaching and find the right future for all their students." This requires concentrating on building solid foundations, planning for the long term, analyzing the needs of customers (pupils), and orienting services to meet their needs. I believe that nonprofit managers should follow the same path.

The Grenfell Towers block disaster in London in 2017, in which over 80 people died and 300 were made homeless, has shown how the community and its own nonprofit organization responded far more swiftly

---

[7] https://hbr.org/2016/10/the-one-type-of-leader-who-can-turn-around-a-failing-school

and sensitively than government at all levels. I believe that nonprofit organizations still provide the most opportunities to work creatively and innovatively in developing positive solutions to tackling the most difficult issues in society and the environment.

About the Authors

Don Macdonald has 10 years of youth and community work experience followed by 30 years' management and consultancy experience, both in the United Kingdom and abroad, with nonprofit and public organizations providing services for disadvantaged groups. During this time he initiated a successful national charity, founded a viable social enterprise, managed social enterprises for large nonprofits and trained social enterprise consultants in Myanmar. Don has provided consultancy, research, coaching, and training, particularly for emerging nonprofits and social enterprises. He is chair of trustees for LFJ, a youth integration nonprofit. He has taught management skills, teaches nonprofit studies at the University of Greenwich and other institutions and he paints and draws.

Charles Oham lectures, consults, researches, and practices social entrepreneurship in the United Kingdom and the developing world. He is a senior lecturer in Social Enterprise at the University of Greenwich. Charles sits on the board of two social enterprises and has worked on projects that address disadvantage using social entrepreneurial and innovation models.

Sue Causton is a management coach, working with public and voluntary sector leaders, managers, and board members. Previously she worked as operations director at a large London housing association, and in youth and community projects in a range of roles. Sue has also worked in Cambodia.

Index

OTHER TITLES IN THE HUMAN RESOURCE MANAGEMENT AND ORGANIZATIONAL BEHAVIOR COLLECTION

- *The Illusion of Inclusion: Global Inclusion, Unconscious Bias, and the Bottom Line* by Helen Turnbull
- *On All Cylinders: The Entrepreneur's Handbook* by Ron Robinson
- *Employee LEAPS: Leveraging Engagement by Applying Positive Strategies* by Kevin E. Phillips
- *Making Human Resource Technology Decisions: A Strategic Perspective* by Janet H. Marler and Sandra L. Fisher
- *Feet to the Fire: How to Exemplify And Create The Accountability That Creates Great Companies* By Lorraine A. Moore
- *HR Analytics and Innovations in Workforce Planning* By Tony Miller
- *Deconstructing Management Maxims, Volume I: A Critical Examination of Conventional Business Wisdom* by Kevin Wayne
- *Deconstructing Management Maxims, Volume II: A Critical Examination of Conventional Business Wisdom* by Kevin Wayne
- *The Real Me: Find and Express Your Authentic Self* by Mark Eyre
- *Across the Spectrum: What Color Are You?* by Stephen Elkins-Jarrett
- *The Human Resource Professional's Guide to Change Management: Practical Tools and Techniques to Enact Meaningful and Lasting Organizational Change* by Melanie J. Peacock
- *Tough Calls: How to Move Beyond Indecision and Good Intentions* by Linda D. Henman

CPSIA information can be obtained
at www.ICGtesting.com
Printed in the USA
LVHW080807150122
708669LV00029B/907